"Randy DonGiovanni is a dynamic young man who has a mission to reach, raise, and release a generation for Jesus Christ. Randy's ability to effectively coach leadership and reach students with real impact has been such a blessing to Resurrection Life Church Rockford. As Randy's senior pastor, we are blessed to have him as our Director of Student and Young Adult ministry and to provide a home base as he travels across the country touching the next generation."

–Pastor Doug Bergsma,
Rockford, Michigan
Resurrection Life Church

"Dedicated, Consistent, Funny, Faithful, Friend are just a few words that describe Randy DonGiovanni. A man committed to the next generation who has provided ministry and leadership to youth and those who lead them for decades. You will be encouraged as you read the pages of this book, and I know you will share its truths with others. As his friend and ministry partner for over twenty years, I give him the highest of recommendations!!"

–Rick Pasquale,
RPM Global CEO

"I have known Randy for many years. I have never met anyone who is more contagious in their enthusiasm for Christ or more passionate to see youth come into a life changing relationship with their Savior. His dedication to keep his hand to the plow over nearly three decades of youth ministry gives him a rare, long term perspective on what will actually work as opposed to what is the latest passing fancy. When you are inspired by his contagious passion and guided by his experience, I know you will be blessed."

—Steve Croft, Associate Pastor,
Rockford, Michigan
Resurrection Life Church

"Randy DonGiovanni is a proven youth specialist. His impact on students can be seen in the lives of thousands of young adults who are chasing their dreams. His ability to connect with the student culture and effectively relate scriptural truths has given him the ability to be a true dream releaser."

—Doug Clay,
General Treasurer of the Assemblies of God

[ir]Relevant
Youth Ministry
Making it Matter

Randy DonGiovanni
with Greg Smith

Black Lake Press
TELL YOUR STORY
BLACKLAKEPRESS.COM

Black Lake Press
TELL YOUR STORY
BLACKLAKEPRESS.COM

Cover design by Greg Smith of Black Lake Studio.

Published by Black Lake Press of Holland, Michigan.
Black Lake Press is a division of Black Lake Studio, LLC.
Direct inquiries to Black Lake Press at
www.blacklakepress.com.

ISBN 978-0-9883373-0-5

Dedication

To the three most influential people in my life:
My wife Lori for always supporting me, motivating me,
and loving me in our journey together.
My mother Alma who always showed me, taught me,
and lived a life of Jesus before me.
My grandfather Frank who was a real example and
role model of Christ to me. Thank you for investing,
enabling, and showing me the love of Christ throughout
my life's journey.

Table of Contents

Acknowledgements

Thanks to:

To My Best Friend–Jesus Christ:

You have given my life purpose. Thank you for coming into my life at the age of eight and helping me never look back. Jesus, thank you for calling me to preach with boldness and your anointing. Jesus, you saw something in me before I was created. You have given me power, authority, and dominion over the enemy. You have given me the gift to preach, teach, and motivate people to the throne room of God. You have given me the gift of eternal life. Thank you for being my Lord, my Savior, and everlasting friend!

My Wife–Lori:

You are the greatest gift God has ever given me. You are the perfect person to put up with me and all my faults. You have driven and pushed me to become the man I am today. Thank you for allowing me to do what God has called us to do. I am forever grateful, and I love you with all of my heart.

You are my partner, confidant, my listener, and best friend for life!

To My Mother–Alma DonGiovanni:

Thank you for always believing in me. You have always pushed me to become better, showing me Jesus at an early age. Mom, thank you for showing me what a godly woman looks like. You are a great role model, and you are a hero to me. You have been the most influential person in my life. You have always viewed me as a great gift from God. You have made me into the person I am today.

To My Father–Francis DonGiovanni (who is with Jesus):

I will always be grateful to you for teaching me early that, through all life experiences, I can stay focused on godly principles. You taught me that I don't need to look or act like the world and what it means to persevere. Thank you for teaching me to make the right choices and be a real man for God through any of life's circumstances.

To My Mother and Father-in-Law–Nina and Frank Coppola:

From the beginning you have supported me, prayed for me, and believed in me. For all the fantastic meals, fun

memories in New York, to the quarters for laundry, thank
you! Thank you for trusting in me and giving me one of the
greatest gifts in life: your daughter.

To My Family–sisters, sisters in law, brothers in law,
nephews, and nieces:

All of you who have given me words of encouragement,
the will to press on, and happiness that only a family can
give. Each one of you has played a valuable part in my life. I
have witnessed many of you push through tough
circumstances and major difficulties. I have watched as the
Lord performed miracles and blessed your lives with His
abundance and provision. No matter the circumstance, you
have trusted God for help, guidance, and wisdom. I have
learned from you how to persevere, stay focused, and to
make the right decisions even when life did not make sense
or seem fair. You have always been there for us, and we are
forever grateful to be in this family.

To My Friends–Rick and Jennifer Pasquale:

You are great friends who have poured into me and
believed in me. You have been friends who saw potential in
me, trusted, and pushed me into becoming who I am today.
It's true when the scripture says "iron sharpens iron so one

man sharpens another." Thank you for always being there for me; I am forever grateful.

To My Best Friends Forever—Geno Levi, Michael Yoder, and Michael Zatta

You have always been there for me. Friends that have been the best brothers anyone could have ever asked for. You are my true brothers in Christ. Thank you for always believing in me and looking past my faults to see what God saw in me. I have known you my entire life, and I believe that God handpicked you to be there for me. You have guided me, taught me, chastened me, given me tough love, and breathed words of hope and encouragement to me. Thank you my spiritual brothers: I am forever grateful.

To My Spiritual Parents, Mentors, and Friends—Robert & Darlene Muirhead:

You have always believed in me, pushed me, disciplined me, and motivated me to be what God had for me. You gave me my first opportunity to be a youth pastor. I was green, raw, and had no idea what I was doing, and yet you gave me a chance. Pastor Muirhead, thank you for the tough love, the time spent over a cup of coffee mentoring, trusting, and pouring Jesus into me. You believed in me even when I didn't believe in myself. Some said you took a risk in hiring a person with no experience, and yet you never treated me like that. You saw something in me from the very beginning. What a great ride we had. Thank you for being my spiritual parents. You both are my heroes! I am forever grateful.

To My Role Models—Doug Bergsma & Steve Croft:

Thank you for believing in me at this point in life when others said I was too old to be effective to this generation of young people. You have shown me grace, faith, and value. You both have given me the opportunity to excel in ministry. I thank you for being my friends.

To My Co-Author and Editors—Greg Smith, Michael Brooks, and Jami Vander Kooi:

Thank you for hearing my heart and making my words come to life.

And a special thanks to all of our youth leaders throughout the past twenty-seven years to the present.

Lori and I are so grateful for all of you who have invested your time, love, prayers, and support to us and every young person you came in contact with. We owe you so much; we could never say "thank you" enough. Without you, our ministries would have never been as powerful or successful.

We are forever indebted to each and everyone of you.

Foreword

As a Pastor, I am very passionate about youth ministry. We dedicate a large portion of our building and revenue to reaching youth. We know that over ninety percent of those who make a decision to serve Christ do so before they reach the age of twenty.

I first met Randy five years ago when he became the youth pastor of a megachurch just a few miles away. I was immediately impressed by his passion to not only reach youth in the church but to also reach those outside the church. We continually watch Randy's ministry, and we see how God continues to use him and that he has God's heart for youth ministry as expressed by Jesus in Matthew 19:14. Randy is not only insightful but his communication skills are also unmatched.

I know that as you read this book, Randy's passion and heart will come through. It is not 'flash' that changes hearts but a strong presentation of the Gospel by someone who knows it, lives it, loves it, and passionately shares it–

someone who will step out of the confines of our buildings and go to where the need is—with an incarnation for youth.

–Pastor Duane VanderKlok, Senior Pastor,

Resurrection Life Church

Grandville, Michigan

Introduction: Let's Make it Matter

Youth ministry isn't working very well in the American Church. Why? Well, it seems to me that our youth ministries ought to have at least three goals:

1. Lead the teens in our care to accept Christ as their savior.
2. Teach them to obey his commands and live as one of his followers.
3. Grow up to become part of and actively participate in his body, the Church.

I didn't make up those goals arbitrarily. They come directly from the Great Commission in Matthew 28:19-20: "Therefore go and make disciples of all nations, baptizing them in the name of the Father and of the Son and of the Holy Spirit, and teaching them to obey everything I have commanded you." Of course we normally think of this command in the context of missions and evangelism. But if it's what we are supposed to do with people down the block or ten thousand miles away, should we not at least be doing it with our own teenagers?

Sure, there are some great youth pastors and some great youth groups. But over the last ten or twenty years, it would be hard to give American youth ministry anything beyond a "C" grade. And that's being generous. Consider some statistics from Josh McDowell's book, The Last Christian Generation (Baker, 2006). These are based on surveys of evangelical "Christian" kids:

- 63% don't believe Jesus is the Son of the one true God
- 58% believe all faiths teach equally valid truths
- 51% don't believe Jesus rose from the dead
- 65% don't believe Satan is a real entity
- 68% don't believe the Holy Spirit is a real entity
- 64% believe if a person is generally good or does enough good things for others they will earn a place in heaven
- 81% believe all truth relates to the individual
- 72% say it's true if it works for you
- 85% of evangelical youth "drop out" of church between 10th-12th grade

Although these statistics are a few years old, survey after survey by other researchers has confirmed the findings. Some say that 50% of the "Millennial" generation (born approximately between 1980 and 2000, also known as Generation Y) is leaving the faith and dropping out of the Church, and some say it's closer to 90%. But they all agree that the slide in American Christianity, which began with their grandparents, the Baby Boomers, and continued with their parents, Generation X, has fallen off a cliff with GenY/the Millennials.

Our churches, despite all the money and energy spent on youth ministry, are failing to fulfill the Great Commission with our own kids.

Where are We Going in American Youth Ministry?

I've been in youth ministry for over twenty-seven years. I plan, Lord willing, on doing youth ministry until I retire. But I can't help but wonder what the landscape of youth ministry will look like in twenty years. Not all of our kids are leaving the Church—but most of them are. A lot of them will come back as they get older, grow up, and settle down—but not all of them will and maybe most of them won't. As our churches become increasingly full of old people, where will the next generation of parents and teens come from?

The easy answer is that we will build relationships with teens outside our churches and bring them in. After all, Jesus' parable about the wedding banquet tells us that if those invited don't come, we should go into the streets and highways and hedges and bring them in. I believe with all my heart that we need to reach the kids who've grown up outside the Church. Our youth programs need to be more evangelistic and outreaching to the kids down the block whose parents don't come to church on Sunday. But I see a few problems with that as our primary strategy to reach the next generation.

First, Jesus also says that those who are faithful with a little are given responsibility over more. We (and I mean all of us, youth pastors, senior pastors, lay leaders, parents, congregation members) haven't produced much fruit with our own kids. Yes, the reasons they are leaving the Church is complex and part of larger trends in society, but we can't use that as an excuse. The reality is that our youth ministry efforts over the last twenty or thirty years didn't find a way to counteract the forces pushing the next generation out the door. If it wasn't our job, our responsibility, to find a solution, then whose was it? We didn't get it done. In fact, some or even a lot of what we did do made the problem worse. If we have failed (yes, I said it) with the children God did give us, can we assume that he will give us more? If Christ wants to reach them he will, but it may not be through our existing youth ministries, programs, and structures.

Second, why would the kids down the block come to our church youth groups? Because of how effective our programs are, how relevant and useful the Church is to them? If what we're doing isn't reaching the kids we already have in our building, what makes us think that it will somehow start working for kids down the block who are another generation further removed from the Church then the kids who grew up in Sunday School? As every boss or coach will tell you, the best predictor of future performance is past performance. Are we going to get better at what we do? Revival?

Third, will that congregation of aging Baby Boomers and some GenX holdouts (the Millennials having fled the coop) fund our positions? Let's tell ourselves the truth: our budgets are supported by the sense of urgency that parents in the congregation feel for their children's spiritual well-being. If (when) we get to the point that our congregations have very few parents of teens, how much priority will be given to funding congregational youth ministry? I'm not saying that adults ten or twenty years from now won't care about the unchurched kids down the block or refuse to fund evangelism efforts. But it will be missionary work, an outreach program. The focus and funding will change.

So, if ten or so years from now we've lost most of the Millennials and have a hard time reaching the unchurched kids down the block from our established churches, where does that leave youth ministry in America? Where are we going?

I think that we will become less youth pastors and more missionaries to youth. Our mission field will be the teens of 2025. Unlike the last twenty or thirty years, our job won't be to reinforce the faith that their parents and the congregation built into them, since their parents will be the generation bailing out of the Church today. The teens of 2025 will have as little familiarity with Christianity and Christian concepts as kids in Europe or Asia do today.

Because of this, the structures and methods of youth ministry in 2025 and beyond will probably be very different than today. The suburban churches we work at now, full of aging Boomers and Xers in 2025, might not (probably won't) appeal to the children of the Millennials. And those churches might not give us big youth rooms, big budgets, and big buses for big retreats and rallies. It very well may require new congregations to reach the children of the Millennials.

But while change is inevitable, the missionary youth ministry of 2025 won't be hopeless. In fact, while the Church in America has only a so-so record of reaching teenagers for Christ over the last thirty years, it has learned a lot about how to reach kids on the mission field. Since the mission field is coming to our neighborhood, we can apply the lessons of missions to 21st century youth ministry. But we'd better do it fast, because we're running out of time.

Two Paths Forward

Why has the American Church been steadily losing its kids over the last ten to twenty years? I won't tell you that it's a simple problem. There are lots of reasons, and the causes are complex. But one stands out in my mind: we've tried too hard to be relevant to youth culture.

That's the opposite of our instincts. It's not obvious or intuitive. Our first reaction has been to reach out to them by adopting and adapting our ministries to "speak their language." We listen to what they want, need, and feel and try to connect to them through their culture.

But that hasn't worked. The harder we try to relate to their culture, the further away they drift. Why?

Yes, missions requires us to learn the language of the people we are trying to reach, but only so that we can speak the Word of God. When we learn the language of youth culture to share a weak message or when we have no real message, it's pointless. We shouldn't be trying too hard to be a hero to teens, to embody their culture. We should be striving to have Christ's character and his full love. If we don't, it doesn't matter whether we dress like they do or get their lingo down. In fact, if we don't clothe ourselves in Christ, it doesn't matter what we say. Paul tells us in 1 Corinthians 13 that we can speak in the tongues of men and angels, but if we don't have love, we are a clanging gong.

We make a big mistake when our goal is to offer them what they think they want. That isn't necessarily, or even often, what they need. Of course, all of us have gaps between our wants and needs. But if adults have a hard time figuring out what is good for us, it's especially true for teens—after all, they're only kids.

We need to have enough confidence in the person of Jesus and the power of the Gospel to bring it to them, whether they ask for it or not.

There are two paths we can take forward. One is to continue to try and be relevant to popular youth culture.

The other path is to be relevant to Christ and his Kingdom. That should be our orientation, our point of reference, our North Star. All of us who are serious about our faith agree that Jesus should be the model for our character and life. Romans 12:2 tells us, "Do not conform to the pattern of this world, but be transformed by the renewing of your mind. Then you will be able to test and approve what God's will is—his good, pleasing and perfect will."

But are we conforming our youth ministries to the patterns of this world? I think that we have, in too many ways, and that is a big part of why we are losing kids to the world. Jesus tells us that we are the salt of the earth, "But if the salt loses its saltiness, how can it be made salty again? It is no longer good for anything, except to be thrown out and trampled underfoot" (Matthew 5:13). Have our models for youth ministry lost their saltiness? Is that part of our problem?

I think that it is time for us to become unashamedly, gloriously irrelevant to popular youth culture.

We need to stop chasing the approval of fifteen year olds. We need to love them and lead them to the source of that love, even if that runs against the current of everything they value. Paul boldly declared that, "I am not ashamed of the gospel, because it is the power of God that brings salvation to everyone who believes: first to the Jew, then to the Gentile." Yes, Paul went to the Gentiles—but only to bring them Christ. He never tried to be relevant in their eyes to their culture. Instead, he brought them what was really relevant.

It's time for us to stop chasing relevance to a decaying culture. The stakes are too high to keep goofing around with trivialities and entertainment. Let's be irrelevant to what is perishing and be relevant to what matters. If we do, we will make our youth ministries really matter once again. That's what this book is about.

Chapter 1

The Gospel is Good Enough

A friend of mine told me an interesting story about how his church hired a new youth pastor. It made me think about what really matters in youth ministry.

Here's how he described the congregation. It was a fairly traditional and conservative church in a suburb of Los Angeles. It sat on the corner of a boulevard that formed the boundary line between "transitional" neighborhoods. On one side of the boulevard, the neighborhoods were made up of primarily middle class, white families who had lived in the area for a couple of generations. The congregation had been there for fifty years, and most of the teenagers in the church were from those neighborhoods. They went to church with their grandparents, who themselves had gotten married in the building when it was new. These teens were surrounded by family and familiarity. They had gone through Sunday school and middle school youth groups. By the time they got to high school, they were well-behaved but mostly bored.

On the other side of the boulevard, the neighborhoods had gradually become more working class. First and second generation Hispanic and Asian immigrants lived there, and there was a growing gang problem. The working class individuals saw the outside of the big, brick church building everyday but very few had ever seen the inside. A few kids from this side of the boulevard had attended a vacation Bible school, and a few of their mothers occasionally attended a women's outreach Bible study. But there was little interest. The congregation had no real relationship with or "relevance" to the folks in these neighborhoods.

Over the previous ten years, several youth pastors had come and gone. Some had been outgoing and dynamic; others had a more pastoral style. All had tried to bridge the gap between the two sides of the boulevard, but the Wednesday night high school group still only attracted a couple of dozen students, almost all of them from the families who had grown up in that congregation.

When another youth pastor resigned and moved on out of frustration and had an ambition to attend seminary and become a senior pastor, the church council decided to really invest in their youth program. They could see that it wasn't serving either side of the boulevard very well and needed new vision and resources to grow. The elders of the church approved a huge budget increase for the youth ministry. They set aside enough money to hire an experienced full-time youth pastor, make major renovations to the youth room, and fund an expansion of their programs. They wanted to "do it right," so they advertised the position on denominational websites and in ministry publications. They wanted someone well-qualified who could make and follow through on a strategic plan to grow the program.

The resumes came in the mail. All of the applicants had at least Bible college training, and some had seminary-level master's degrees in youth ministry. In the interviews, they described all the programs they would launch, and all the structures and process they would put into place. They proposed plans for bands, small groups, movies, outings, retreats, canvassing, mission trips, outreach cafés, sports leagues—a catalogue of every idea in youth ministry over the last decade or so. Each applicant assured the hiring committee that their strategy would be a success by producing growth.

But the senior pastor and one or two of the elders felt a pause in their spirits. They couldn't put their finger on the problem, but they felt the Holy Spirit telling them that they hadn't found the right person yet. They asked their prayer partners to lift the search up to the Lord and lead them to the right person.

There was one other applicant, but they had not taken his resume seriously. While everyone else who had applied for the job was in their twenties, this guy was in his mid fifties. While they all had at least a college degree, he hadn't graduated from high school. While they all had previous experience in paid youth positions, he had been a house painter and handyman for most of his career. He had become a Christian when his own kids were in middle school, had brought them to the church he got saved in (not the one he was applying for the job at), and became a parent volunteer in the high school program there.

But now this man (let's call him Jim) had built his painting business and had been able to buy a few rental houses. While he wasn't wealthy, he was in a position to step away from his business and start a second career. And he couldn't think of anything he wanted to do more than work with high school students as a youth pastor.

The senior pastor felt the Lord leading him to bring Jim in for an interview. He convinced the executive committee to give him half an hour to meet Jim and hear what he had to say. Some of those on the committee were skeptical, but they respected the pastor enough to let him set up the meeting.

Jim came into the council room with only two items in his hand. The council asked him to share his vision and plan for growing the youth ministry, should he be given the position.

"I dropped out of high school to work. I don't have any formal training. Financially, I don't need this job. I could just keep running my rentals and my painting business. But I want to serve Christ by serving teenagers."

"I'm not going to tell you that I have a big strategic plan for this youth ministry. In fact, the only strategic plan I have is this." He held up the first item, a large, well-worn and heavily-marked up study Bible. "I believe in this book. I believe that it's enough, and I will follow it and teach it to the kids every time I'm in front of them."

He then held up the second item, a six-page list of names and phone numbers. He handed it to the chairman of the committee and explained.

"This is a list of all the kids I've worked with as a youth volunteer over the last five years. I haven't cherry-picked; every one of them is there. I've put down their parents' names and phone numbers. I have tried to represent Jesus to these kids. You can call any of them, as many as you want, and ask them any question that you want. I haven't been perfect, but I have nothing to hide."

Jim continued, "If you give me the chance, I will do everything I can to share the Gospel with every kid within walking distance of this building."

When I heard this story, I thought about the apostle Paul, and something that he said in 1 Corinthians 2:

> *And so it was with me, brothers and sisters. When I came to you, I did not come with eloquence or human wisdom as I proclaimed to you the testimony about God. For I resolved to know nothing while I was with you except Jesus Christ and him crucified. I came to you in weakness with great fear and trembling. My message and my preaching were not with wise and persuasive words, but with a demonstration of the Spirit's*

power, so that your faith might not rest on human
wisdom, but on God's power. (1 Corinthians 2:1-5)

Paul wasn't cool. He wasn't successful in ministry because he was charismatic. He wasn't funny or particularly well-dressed. He didn't fit in with the pop culture of his day. He wasn't persuasive because he was a great speaker. He was brilliant, but that's not why people responded to him. In fact, his critics said he was too mild-mannered and didn't have the right qualifications.

But what Paul did have was the Gospel, and the character of Christ. He didn't try to enhance or add to or "sell" the gospel through clever marketing or packaging. He had no strategic plan except to follow the Spirit and preach Christ every chance he got, to anyone he met.

He said, "For to me, to live is Christ and to die is gain" (Philippians 1:21).

Some of Paul's worst critics were the "super apostles," at least that's what Paul sarcastically called them. They were professional ministers, who had the equivalent of university training and all the right connections throughout the Roman world. They traveled through the churches of the Eastern Mediterranean and charged money to preach and teach. They had letters of recommendation from all sorts of important people and made fun of Paul because he didn't carry such letters. He responded to them by arguing that the only resume he needed was the fruit that his ministry had borne in the lives of the people he had ministered to:

> ...do we need, like some people, letters of recommendation to you or from you? You yourselves are our letter, written on our hearts, known and read by everyone. You show that you are a letter from Christ, the result of our ministry, written not with ink but with the Spirit of the living God, not on tablets of stone but on tablets of human hearts. (2 Corinthians 3:1-3).

When I heard of how Jim walked into that interview, I wished that every youth pastor in America could be so clear and bold. I wish all of us would be able to print a list of all the kids we had worked with and say, "Here is my resume. These are my qualifications." I wish that all of us could say that God's Word was our ministry plan. There is nothing wrong with education or studying youth ministry in college or seminary. There is also nothing wrong with making program plans. But I wish that more of us really believed that the Gospel was good enough and strong enough to stand on its own without us having to help it along.

That's what we do when we layer a whole bunch of activities and entertainment on top of God's Word. We tell ourselves that all of this will attract kids so that we can share the Gospel. But the Gospel doesn't need help. It has stood for 2,000 years, through a hundred generations of believers. It's not our job to package or market or sell it. Our task is to share it and let the Holy Spirit work through it to soften hearts and change lives.

Jim got the job. He took some of the money the council had offered for renovations to the youth room and gave it a fresh coat of paint and added a few amenities. But he didn't build an entertainment center or youth night club. It was essentially just a big room. Every Wednesday night, they did some ice breakers and played a few games to burn off energy. Then he sat the students down on the floor, took out his Bible, and taught for at least half an hour. He walked them through parts of the Bible the kids had never even heard of.

And a funny thing happened. From a dozen bored church kids and a handful of kids from the wrong side of the boulevard, a large and dynamic youth ministry grew. Within a year, Jim had hundreds of kids coming on Wednesday nights. In fact, there were so many, and so many from troubled backgrounds, Jim had to use part of his budget each week to hire private security guards because a few gang members brought guns to youth group. He had altar calls, and baptized dozens in a month. Within a few years, Jim was closer to sixty than fifty, and his ministry was reaching so many kids from the area that the traditional church on that corner could barely cover the logistics and costs.

Jesus doesn't need a cool young youth pastor with the latest haircut, glasses, and T-shirt.

The gospel doesn't need to be properly marketed to succeed. And ministry is ultimately measured with results, not resumes. If we believe that the Gospel is good enough to change a kid's life, let's share it boldly without embellishment and then get out of the way to see what God is going to do.

Chapter 2

Randy's Story

Jesus got my attention when I was eight years old.

As a child, I was happy to spend my summer nights playing stickball in the streets of South Washington, Pennsylvania, just south of Pittsburgh. My parents had separated due to some wrong choices my father had made. My mom, my three sisters, and I moved in with my grandparents on South Main Street, a heavily Italian influenced neighborhood. For three-and-a-half years they raised me and shaped my character forever.

My grandparents and my mother brought me and my three sisters to their Pentecostal church, where the hellfire and brimstone preaching, praise and worship songs, and outpourings of the Spirit were all delivered in a mixture of Italian and English. The same people got "saved" every single Sunday. If you went to a bowling alley or to a movie on Saturday, you repented for it the next morning. If Jesus were to return then, and you did these things, you certainly would not make it into heaven. My friends and I got bored with it often, and sometimes we'd belly-crawl under the pews while the adults gave it up for God. When we got caught, it was our turn to repent. I went to Sunday school in the church basement, which was a dark and scary place. The other boys and I would spend most of our time down there ignoring the teacher and talking about what we had done on Saturday night, for which we were not sufficiently repentant.

My grandfather made a bigger impact in my life than anyone else. I admired him so much, even as a little boy without my own dad around. Shortly after my grandmother immigrated from Italy to the United States, passing through the famous stop on Ellis Island in New York harbor, she met my grandfather, who had been raised in Pennsylvania. He was a physically small man, but he did with me all the things my dad wasn't around to do. He taught me to ride a bike and catch a fish. But I don't think he ever knew just how much I was watching him and learning to become the man that I am from his example.

Some days, I would work in his barber shop, shining customers' shoes while he cut their hair. I watched and listened as he shared the Gospel every chance he got. He would be snipping away at loose hairs and shaving the scruff off men's faces and almost casually ask, "Do you know Jesus?"

"Yeah, yeah, Frank," the guy in the chair would say as he rolled his eyes. "I know him."

"No, really," Grandpap would press. "Do you know Him?"

Some customers would play along, humoring him until their haircut was over and they could get away. But not all of them. Some listened, and some of those conversations led to changed lives. Grandpap was a genuinely humble man. That's why he turned the conversation to Jesus: he didn't think he had anything of value to offer himself, other than a haircut and the Good News.

As I literally sat at his feet with my shoeshine rag in my hand, God planted deep within me an evangelistic seed.

It would take years for it to break the surface and bloom, but my grandfather did more to shape and enrich my life than anyone else. He always said he wanted me to be "better" than he was—"You can do it, Randy, you're better than I am!" Well, I may have preached to more people in my ministry career than he did in his barber shop, but I have never been a better man than he was. I can't be.

One evening when I was eight, I was sitting in my grandparents' house watching the famous coach of the Dallas Cowboys, Tom Landry, give his Christian testimony on TV. Who knows how God works in the mind and heart of an eight-year-old? But that night, as an NFL coach explained the gospel on a big cabinet TV (without remote control to change the channel), it made sense to me. I asked the Lord to come into my heart. When I told my mother, she said that I no longer had the DNA of my earthly father in my blood. That DNA had led him to wrong choices. Mom said that my body now had the DNA of Jesus Christ. I was a little copy of him, and I was free to serve and enjoy him forever.

A few years later, Dad got in a really bad car accident and almost died. As the EMTs loaded him up on the gurney and rushed him to the hospital, he made a promise to God. He vowed to give his life to God if the Lord would save him. God rescued him in the emergency room, and he didn't forget his promise. He was in the hospital a long time recuperating, but when he came home he was a changed man. Some changes were immediate: he quit drinking and smoking—cold turkey—and began to read his Bible every day. Other changes took a long while: he was still really tough on me—heck, I'd say borderline verbally abusive—but things began to move in a new direction. I watched my dad change from a man who had hardly anything to do with the church to a man who carried his Bible to work with him every morning. I began to get to know him as a father, and he began to get involved in my life. He didn't attend all my extracurricular activities and sporting events, but we became a family again.

Like Grandpap, both of my parents were hairdressers. Ironically, I'm the only bald man in the family. For all their influence on my heart and spirit, I often find myself wishing they had thought to anoint my head as well.

As I entered my junior year of high school, my family left the Italian-American pentecostal church. We began attending an Assemblies of God congregation. It was there, in 1976 during my junior year, that God called me into youth ministry. I was still just a student myself, but the call he placed on my heart then and there confirmed what grandmother and other people had spoken into my life as I was growing up. I knew God wanted me to grow up and reach students.

During my high school years, the churches I attended went through three youth pastors in four years. The chaos and inconsistency bothered me. I believed that these youth pastors were supposed to be God-given mentors and that the congregational leaders were wise. So why did we rotate youth pastors every year? So as much as I felt called, I was scared.

After high school, I attended Valley Forge Christian College in Phoenixville, Pennsylvania. I studied secondary education with a minor in Bible and graduated in 1982. Afterwards, I got a job with that college, teaching physical education and coaching soccer. I started working on a master's degree in secondary education. That's when I met Lori, my wife-to-be and got engaged. Nine years had gone by since I felt called into youth ministry as a high school junior, and I hadn't done anything to move toward a youth ministry career.

One morning at Lori's church, a guest speaker preached a sermon that stirred the passion for the long-avoided call in my heart. Passing rows of people, I went up to the altar for prayer. I knew the moment had arrived to stop being a fleeing Jonah and go to my Ninevah: youth ministry. At the altar, I said yes to God's call, having no idea what youth ministry was going to look like or how I'd even get there at that point in my career.

I returned to Valley Forge, waiting on the Lord to speak, and he did. The Lord told me that I was going to get a call from a pastor in March and start as a youth pastor in May. As I made preparations to wrap up my time at Valley Forge, I called my soccer team together to tell them the news. Visiting the college at the time was a preacher named Mark Muirhead. Mark's dad was the pastor of a church in Battle Creek, Michigan who had been desperately seeking a youth pastor. Mark saw the way I coached and mentored my players. He called his dad and said, "I just found your youth pastor." And just as the Lord said, Mark's father called me that March and offered me the position.

I spent eleven years at Battle Creek First Assembly of God. It was my first youth ministry, and I could write whole chapters about what I learned there. I found my call, I made mistakes, and I developed my gifts. When the pastor who hired me resigned, I did as well. I loved that man, and I knew that no matter how great the next pastor might be, the ministry we built together would change. It was the closing of a chapter, and time to start a new one.

Six months later, I followed that pastor to his new church. After fourteen months there, Lori and I felt like we had been living away from our family in Pennsylvania for too long and needed some time there to rest and reboot. For a season, we did reconnect with our roots in Pennsylvania, but God opened another opportunity that we couldn't turn down. We returned to Michigan, and spent the next two and a half years serving a ministry called Youth Alive for the Michigan District of the Assemblies of God in Farmington Hills, Michigan. In 2001, we moved to Grand Rapids, Michigan, and I served First Assembly of God as Director of Student Ministries until 2009. In that last year there, I felt a new call in my life. God put it into my heart that I needed to enlarge my youth ministry to reach more kids and mentor other youth pastors.

I realized that the Millennial Generation (GenY) in America was a mission field. The next generation of American kids needed missionaries, and I could be one of them. I sought the prayers and advice of wise and experienced people around me, and they helped me launch RandyDon Ministries.

At the time of this writing, I was hired as Director of Student and Young Adult Ministry at Resurrection Life Church in Rockford, Michigan. The great thing about where I am now is that this church allows me to travel as a youth evangelist who speaks all over the country, and I spend about two weekends a month on the road. I think the kids in my youth group think it's cool that I am reaching others just like them. They like hearing stories about what God is doing in their generation.

My wife is a nurse. She is a compassionate person, who genuinely cares for people's souls as well as their bodies. Our marriage has been built on faith, hope, and trust. My wife has always been my "steady." We will be married twenty-six years this November (2012).

At the moment, I'm fifty-three years old. People ask me all the time how a guy my age can be relevant to youth culture. I respond that I'm not trying to be relevant to their culture; I'm calling them to be relevant for Christ. I think that the age of the youth pastor is irrelevant to youth ministry. I know great youth pastors that are older than I am and boring and ineffective ones that are twenty-one years old. I don't do "old." Culture has changed, but the heart of the kids hasn't. Their hurts and needs are no different than mine were when I was their age. Only the music, fashions, and technology has changed. But that's all superficial stuff.

I care about and work to connect with their hearts.

Ever since that night I heard coach Tom Landry give his testimony on TV when I was eight, I have believed that Jesus' Kingdom matters. I know that he has used people like my grandfather to make it matter to me. Youth ministry is not a transitional or temporary career for me. I am in this for life, and I will keep making it matter to kids as long as the Lord lets me. I hope you will do the same.

Chapter 3

It's Not About Us

It's not about us.

We all know and believe that, but sometimes we get so wrapped up in our ministry that we forget that it's supposed to be youth ministry. We get the means and ends backwards, or we let what we want overwhelm what the teens need. Sometimes the switch happens so quietly that we don't even notice when it's no longer about them.

I was talking about this with a former youth pastor, and he told me about a time when he let that kind of reversal happen to him. He was right out of college in his first full time ministry job. He had a small youth ministry and was working hard to care for the kids he had while reaching new ones in the community. He read youth ministry books and websites, looking for ideas for how to build his program. His heart was in the right place, and he was trying to do the right thing.

To help him sharpen his skills, the church paid for him to go to a national youth ministry conference. It was on the other side of the country, and he was excited to fly there and be around thousands of others like himself. He'd never been to a conference like this before, and he was impressed by all the speakers and workshops. The people up on stage were youth ministry superstars, and he could see why. They were passionate, creative, and good at sharing their compelling visions for making a difference in the lives of students. He realized that he wanted to be like them, to be successful in ministry and recognized for it. He daydreamed about someday writing and speaking about how much he had accomplished in his ministry.

One of the keynote speakers stood out in my friend's mind. His talk was about "thinking big." He argued that many youth pastors dreamed too small. They needed bigger ideas, on a bigger scale, with bigger plans, to do bigger things for a big God. Go big or go home! You've probably heard motivational speeches like this before, but my friend hadn't. Away from home at his first national conference, his eyes were full of stars and his heart started beating faster.

The speaker told stories about how he had taken a sleepy little ministry and built it into a nationally known program. My friend remembers one in particular. Before this speaker came to his church, fundraising was done in the traditional way—candy sales, car washes, etc. The kids would raise a few thousand dollars for camp, and everyone was satisfied. But this speaker had bigger dreams. He was determined to scale his program up and take ten times more kids that summer on an international trip. The group would never be able to raise enough money using their traditional methods. So the speaker came up with the idea of booking a contemporary Christian superstar to come to their town and do a concert. He spent most of a year negotiating with agents, booking a big venue, executing a marketing plan, and working with ticket vendors. He had a real knack as a concert promoter and developed key contacts in the music and promotional industries. He got to meet the artist and go onstage during the concert to show a video about his ministry and the trip they were raising money for. It was a huge success. The concert sold out, and made enough of a profit to fund the trip. The speaker became well-known and was asked to speak at national conferences.

Sitting in the thirty-second row of the keynote session, my friend decided right there that he would never again dream too small. He was only a year out of college and working with his first small youth group, but he promised himself that from that point on, he would do everything on a bigger scale. He would think big, plan big, get big. He would make a big difference for God in youth ministry. On the plane going home, he filled a notebook with ideas, and when he got back, he shared all these big ideas with his senior pastor and leaders. They were thrilled, and they committed to help him do great things.

Telling me about it years later, he said that conference marked a turning point for him. While he never became a superstar youth pastor, he did accomplish some things. But while his group grew, in his own heart it became a means to an end. It was subtle, and he didn't notice it at first. He believed that he wanted his ministry to grow so it would have a bigger impact for Christ, but the emphasis was on bigger impact. Without realizing it, his ministry had become a vehicle for his own ambitions and ego. He didn't just want to reach kids, he wanted to be known for reaching kids. While he never admitted it to himself, it became about him. The kids became his career, the path that would get him book deals and put him on a youth ministry stage. And even as he built his program, his heart really wasn't in it. When he realized that the program at his church would never become big enough to be famous, he got discouraged and left youth ministry.

None of us sets out to be an egomaniac. But it can happen without us realizing it. Somewhere in the effort to make our ministry effective and build our career (after all, we do have families to provide for), we can start to care more about ourselves than the kids we are working with. We don't just want to be good at what we do, we want to be great—and we want to be recognized for our greatness. Youth ministry becomes our business, and the kids become our customers. And sometimes it works: we become successful and famous youth pastors.

But if our heart is in the wrong place, then we have lost our way. God will not be pleased, and we'll have little joy in what we do.

Let me suggest four ways that I see us sometimes making our youth ministries about us:

1. **We want to be liked, even loved.** Who doesn't want to be liked? Someone who doesn't care about the affection and admiration of those he leads probably has too hard of a heart to be a great leader. But being liked has its limits. We should never put it ahead of doing the right thing, even if it won't make us popular with the kids or their parents or the congregation. While Paul did say that, "Each of us should please our neighbors for their good, to build them up" (Romans 15:2), when he was criticized for his leadership decisions, he asked, "Am I now trying to win the approval of human beings, or of God? Or am I trying to please people? If I were still trying to please people, I would not be a servant of Christ" (Galatians 1:10). When we value the opinion of others more than the opinion of God, or when we want the kids to come to our ministry because of us, it's no longer about Christ.

2. **We want job security.** Let's be real: we have to provide for our families. Pretending that we don't care about that isn't noble; it's just dishonest. As professional youth pastors, we have a responsibility to serve those who employ us and sign our paychecks. But we have a greater responsibility to Christ. The

congregation may pay us every two weeks and evaluate us every year, but Jesus will ultimately judge our ministry and give us our eternal reward. When we have clear direction from the Lord about something in our ministry, we cannot ignore it just because it might jeopardize our career. In fact, if we are working in a church where obeying Christ might cost us our job, then we're working in the wrong church. But we can't be reckless about these choices. Not every idea and ambition and impulse is from the Lord. We should seek and accept spiritual accountability from our elders, other staff, and ministry partners. We should have a circle of colleagues and friends who can check our motives. Sometimes they tell us that we're going in the wrong direction. But there will be times in our ministry career when we have to be willing to jeopardize our security to do the right thing. We have plenty of examples of standing up for our convictions regardless of the cost, from Jesus himself onward. I hope that you don't have to make this kind of choice, but if you do, remember that your ministry is ultimately not about you and your needs.

3. We design the program around our desires.
It can be tempting to build a youth ministry that's fun for us to lead. If your students are a mostly captive audience (because their parents make them attend), you can find yourself picking the activities and planning trips that appeal to you. Of course, a chef will tend to cook what he likes. It's not the end of the world if you choose to make the bus stop at your favorite fast food place on the group's way back from the retreat. What worries me more is that we might unconsciously favor methods and build programs in order to provide us with a certain lifestyle or job description. A youth pastor with a short attention span might build a ministry that is full of activity but short on consistent relationships. Or another youth pastor, who is bored in his position and loves to travel, might plan one trip after another, regardless of whether they are producing real results in the teens. I agree that any pastor ought to lead with his spiritual gifts and personality and customize a program to fit his identity. But what I'm talking about is something much more serious. You should never bend your youth ministry into your dream job just because you can. Then it really is about you. Take a hard look at the hours you

keep, the number and type of trips you plan for the group, and the program style. Ask and honestly answer this question: "How much of my ministry is really planned for me?"

4. **We use youth ministry as a stepping stone.** Some youth pastors don't really want to be doing youth ministry. They want to pastor adults or become senior pastors or some other position higher up the church staff food chain. These kind of youth pastors see their job as an entry-level position. They figure that if they put a couple of years into it, they can get a promotion or at least use the youth ministry on their resume. They are auditioning for bigger and better things. Their heart is not really invested with the teens in the group, and so they will never achieve everything possible with that group of teens. Youth ministry is a calling all its own, a life-long calling. It's not just for young pastors who need to get experience before moving up the ladder to working with grown-ups. If it's your calling, you will find satisfaction and success in it through your whole ministry career.

If we're going to make our ministries matter, they can't be about us. We are there to serve, to give ourselves first to Christ, then to the kids. The more we pour of ourselves into it, without making it about us, the better off everyone will be.

Chapter 4

Destiny Determines Identity

One of the cruelest things that the world teaches kids today is that their identity determines their destiny, that their past and present will determine their future. In other words, where they came from and where they are today creates an inescapable trajectory for their life. Kids become discouraged, believing that their parents, ethnic background, class, neighborhood, and subculture all conspire to lock them into a life with no real choices.

I believe this is backwards. It's not our past that defines us, it's our future.

1 Peter 2:9-10 tells us:

> ...[We] are a chosen people, a royal priesthood, a
> holy nation, God's special possession, that you
> may declare the praises of him who called you out
> of darkness into his wonderful light. Once you

were not a people, but now you are the people of God; once you had not received mercy, but now you have received mercy. (1 Peter 2:9-10)

In other words, God not only has a plan for our future, but he also has a role for us in his Kingdom.

We are not to understand our identity from the perspective of our past but from this future glory.

Our challenge is to help students see that God has a purpose for them and that this purpose gives their life meaning, despite whatever limits their past has put upon them—even if they come from a broken home or they have been wounded throughout their short lives. None of that ultimately defines who they can become in Christ. It is not their birth that sets the course for their eternity, but their rebirth. They belong to him.

The goal of youth ministry isn't to be relevant to who kids are now; it's to be relevant to who they are becoming in Christ. One of our goals as we work with students is to help them grasp that the circumstances of their pasts matter less than what God has in store for their futures. We must make what is to come matter more than what has been.

The kids you work with are not lost and hopeless. Kids are never spelled L-O-S-E-R. Instead of writing them off, we need to help them grasp the destiny that Christ has prepared for them.

A student that I worked with, we'll call him Jake, shared how he learned to look forward, not backwards, to understand his life's purpose. When he wrote this, he was a sophomore in high school.

"My life was confusing as far as I remember. My parents got divorced when I was two or three, so it caused me to only see my dad on the weekends and spend the weekdays with my mom. Not only was it tough on them, it's been tough on me. I never understood what happened, so I just got used to the fact that my parents were divorced. I know a few times, I would get upset and wish I was a "normal kid" who could go home and find his mom and dad together and happy, but it never happened.

"Around the age of eight, I began to realize my mom was acting different. She wasn't herself. As I got older, I found out my mom was an alcoholic. That was probably the toughest thing in my life. Along with that, it was hard to see my mom be who she was, then later that night, see her drunk and be completely someone else. Around March of 2007, my sister had a baby, so I got to be an uncle. But the baby ended up passing away two months later of something I didn't even want to learn about. My mom would use his death as an excuse for her drinking.

"Throughout the years, I remember I would be leaving for school and I would ask my mom not to drink for that one night, and still I would come home and find my mom drunk. It seemed like my mom just didn't love me. She wouldn't even come home sometimes until 2 a.m. or even 5 a.m., and fights would occur with foul language.

"And along with that, I would take my anger out on my dad, who didn't even deserved it. He was always there for me, along with my stepmom. Even my stepdad was too.

"Being around the housing environment I lived in, I began to pick up a life of sin. I started doing things and saying things that honestly nobody should ever do, but it was a way to take away anger and pain.

"Then after my siblings moved out, me, my mom, and stepdad moved into a better neighborhood where I wouldn't be surrounded by bad influences and, basically, sin. At least a few weeks or a month after moving there, my friend told me about a local youth group, the ROCK. I didn't know what this place was at all, I thought it was a place to go and hang out. Then I got there and it was like a church service, and I was like, 'What is this?'

"I started going weekly, and I started to change my actions and attitude after months. Then, I was asked to start playing bass guitar with them for their worship team. I'd always wanted to be in a band, so I decided I would.

"At this point, my mom was still an alcoholic. It was getting worse, and I didn't know what to do. It was the summer of 2011 that I prayed to God for my mom. I asked Him if he would help her and make her notice the mistakes she was making. A week later, my mom signed into a rehabilitation center. And it was at that moment I started getting more connected to God. I remember her telling me and my brother and it was a moment of awe. I can't even remember my feelings but I'm sure I was an incredibly happy kid—who wouldn't be? That whole summer I started getting more connected to my youth group, and I started going to meetings and a series of classes we have called School of Rock. We have a series called WAR during every summer—an awesome time to get into my Bible and get into the Word.

"That summer was life-changing and exciting. It was a great time, but when I went back to school, the pressure was right there. Kids were telling me to do stuff, but I never went into temptation or peer pressure. I stayed away from what could've happened. And throughout that year, I was getting more attached to God again. People were there praying for me, and I knew I had to live my life for Him.

"2012 was a huge year in my life. I started talking to God more and more, especially when I started getting to know Him. I got into my Bible a lot more and started going to Sunday services. Each week, the Holy Spirit filled me more and more. I still made mistakes I wish I could have taken back, but God passed those. I knew He still loved me, because He has a love that will not fail me. In August of 2012, I accepted Jesus as my personal Savior and started a relationship with Him. I was saved. Weeks before that, I got so much more connected to God, and it's amazing. I love it.

"My attitude changed a lot more. I still get mad at my dad, but there's a deep love there too. Now I'm playing guitar for both youth group and the main church team. I've been talking to God, seeing if being a worship leader is what He wants me to do. I'm excited about what God has planned. I love worshiping Him, and I love leading people into worship. My mom still has her troubles, but she's getting better. Of course, as I said before, I've been praying and talking to God a lot more, and I've just been telling Him thanks for the blessings He has given me in my life. God has the power to do anything; with Him, nothing is impossible."

Jake discovered that what God has planned for us and where He can take us, is far more important than where we've been and what we've done. God redeems and restores. That is what is relevant to Him, and that's the relevance we need to incorporate into youth ministry.

Culturally "Relevant" youth ministry wants to meet kids where they are. Culturally "IrRelevant" youth ministry, what this book is about, wants to meet kids where they are going.

Mikayla was a student who was struggling to make sense of who she was. As I sat with her one night, she told me her story. She had been adopted at a very young age, and now had anger issues, low self esteem, and just longed for someone to love her. She began to tell me how she didn't want to live—how she didn't feel any self worth and how she didn't see how God could or would love her for what she had become and what she had done.

As we sat there talking, I began to ask her a few questions: *Do you know what it means to be adopted? Do you know who your biological mother is? How long have you been in the home you are now? Don't you realize how much you new parents love you? What kind of friends do you have?* It was apparent that she was confused and looking for someone to just spend time with her—someone who was really interested in who she was and how to get her onto the right road so she could discover how much God loves her. I asked her if I could give her an assignment and then could talk again in a few days. I gave her a few questions I wanted her to answer for me over the next week or so.

The questions were simple, but designed to help her see herself from a different perspective: *How do you see yourself? What kinds of talents do you have? How do others see you? What kind of positive things can you bring to the table? How do you think other young people respect you?*

A few days went by and we sat again in my office. We began to discuss the questions I had given her. She was very different this time. Her demeanor had changed, and her focus was a little different. She had all kinds of answers. The more we discussed the questions and answers, the more she began to discover who she was and who she was not. She began to see that she was valuable and yet torn because she belittled herself as a nobody. After a few months she began to see her value and how God poured into her life.

Each day, each week, each month her sense of destiny in Christ became stronger. She blossomed into a young lady that embraced the love of God. Her relationship with her parents changed. Her relationship with her brother and sister changed. Her peers began to respect her in a whole new light. Her self esteem grew stronger. God did a great work in her by letting her future define her identity, not the other way around. Today, this young lady who wanted to take her life now sits in our youth service looking for someone that she can share Christ with. She now sees her purpose. Her eyes are ever looking for someone she can reach out to.

Do you want to make your youth ministry matter? Instead of reducing Christ to a pop culture icon or an excuse to entertain students by reveling in their past and present, introduce them to a future they cannot imagine. This is foolish irrelevance to a perishing world, but to a student who discovers that they are set to inherit an imperishable crown, it is the most relevant thing they could hear.

Chapter 5

Follow Jesus, Not Pop Culture and Trends

A few years ago, a hilarious video was floating around on YouTube. It was a spoof of a hipster youth pastor, "Ignatius, the Ultimate Youth Pastor," who was a caricature (exaggerated for laughs) of so much that is wrong with youth ministry today. The set up in the video is that a mainstream church needed a guest speaker for their student ministry and booked a celebrity youth pastor. The guy shows up, and immediately, there are four obvious problems. First, he cares only about popular culture and style—he wants the kids to be impressed that he is cooler than they are. He's got carefully and expensively disheveled hair, skinny jeans, a graphic tee, and a trendy messenger bag. Second, there is no Bible in his messenger bag or in his message. It's all edgy stories, hip illustrations, and multimedia extravaganzas. Third, he's an unteachable diva. He thinks of himself as a rockstar and his ministry time as a performance. When older and more experienced church leaders question or instruct him, he brushes them off as un-hip old people who don't "get" the way things are done today. Finally, the kids don't actually get anything of value from his ministry. He fails in the most basic task of youth ministry: to minister to young people.

A couple of months ago, I sat with some friends and laughed at the Ignatius video again. We all thought it was funny, but it made us uncomfortable because we realized that it was making fun of a real problem. While the video is an over-the-top satire, it got too close to things we had all actually seen in the church at one time or another. We can joke about this and laugh about bad attempts at "relevant" youth ministry, but when we unpack what's behind the punchline at the heart of the joke, we find that we really have something to talk about.

What does it mean to be culturally relevant to a generation(s) that is constantly changing and being defined by popular culture?

And is it wrong to want to be "relevant" to our kids by following these trends?

First, let me define "popular culture." By that, I mean the mainstream values, music, styles, lifestyle media, behaviors, and language promoted by the mass media aimed at kids between their "tweens" and their early twenties. There are a couple of things we should notice about that culture. First, it's celebrity obsessed. Kids are looking for role models, and the pop culture media supplies them so it can sell the products these celebrities endorse. Second, youth popular culture plays on natural teenage rebellion. Teens have always had a rebellious streak, going back to Adam and Eve's son Cain. The media pushes kids' rebellious buttons by offering a culture that allows them to distinguish themselves from their parents' generation. It always has an element of anger and antagonism and secrecy to it. Third, it manipulates teenage emotions to sell products without offering anything of lasting value.

As missionaries to youth, of course we should try to learn their language and adopt some of their styles. Go ahead and wear a graphic tee, and swap out your backpack for a messenger bag if you think it will help your relationship with the kids. You can even ride a skateboard to church if it makes you feel better. But when youth pastors make following popular culture their primary goal, their ministry will take on the trappings of popular culture that I mentioned in the last paragraph. They will adopt a celebrity mindset and try to impress the students rather than building a genuine relationship with them (like Ignatius did in the video). Second, their ministry won't help build unity between the generations within the church and home, but will stoke teenage rebellion. I've seen youth pastors do things to antagonize the parents or adults in the church just for the sake of appearing cool to the kids. And finally, a youth pastor who takes his marching orders from popular culture rather than Christ will manipulate the kids to build his program instead of allowing the Holy Spirit to lead.

Again, I don't care what shoes you wear or how you cut your hair. If you like being contemporary and that's authentic for you, so be it (not having any hair myself, maybe I've got a bit of a chip on my shoulder). But if being "relevant" to kids means nothing more than wearing the right clothes and glasses and having the latest hairstyle—and making Jesus and the Word a secondary consideration—then I want nothing to do with it. Kids need, and I believe that they really want, an authentic leader, so if all the hipster hair styles and graphic tees aren't who you really are (it certainly isn't me), then don't wear them. They'll see right through you, and your ministry will fail miserably.

Yes, we are in a time where we want things quickly—and that includes "success" in youth ministry. But impatience can lead us to take shortcuts by trying to relate our message to pop culture rather than trying to relate the kids to Christ. We are tempted to tread lightly on the truth so we don't offend.

I've heard this generation called a "microwaveable generation looking for cafeteria-style Jesus."

If we assume this, we have a tendency to water down the Word, hoping we don't turn kids off to the gospel and lose our numbers. It becomes more important to us to be seen as hip, trendy, and cool than to be seen as seriously following Christ against the grain of the world. If we just take the time to sit down with the these kids, we realize that we've sorely underestimated and undervalued their desire for the truth.

One of the worst temptations facing youth pastors today is to copy the style of some successful and well-known youth program in another city. We hear about some youth pastor who grew a huge program very quickly and try to figure out what he or she did. We latch onto the superficial elements: clothes, the room, music, whatever. Those are easy to replicate. So we get a new wardrobe, learn some new catchphrases, redecorate our youth center, and get some new media elements. But too often, we look out of place. Maybe those stylistic elements were truly authentic for the pastor and church that created them, and they fit well into that local community. But we force something on ourselves and our local congregation that feels weird. We dress ourselves and our ministry up and pretend it's something that it's not. And then we're surprised when it fails.

Over the years, I've seen all the changing stylistic models for youth ministry. At one time, it was sports-based. So churches built gymnasiums for the youth in order to reach the kids with basketball and volleyball. That fizzled as schools did away with physical education and focused more on team sports for the athletic kids. They used up all their energy at practice and didn't have the time or energy for church basketball leagues. Meanwhile, the non-athletic kids spent their free time playing video games. The last thing they wanted was to choose up sides and play basketball at youth group.

So churches started building video game stations in youth centers. That was supposed to attract and engage the youth. For a variety of reasons, it didn't. Sure, some of them played their favorite games when they got to youth group, but many were burned out by hours of play at home. And when they did play it distracted and entertained more than it engaged and evangelized.

I've seen youth ministry in America chase trend after trend. I've seen churches invest heavily in the big event or concert model. It reached some kids, but then I've seen others reached when churches flipped and went with a small group model. I've seen churches build what were essentially Christian nightclubs to attract teenagers, and I've seen them build coffee houses. I've seen mission-trips made the focus of the program, and I've seen it be retreats and fun outings. The pendulum is always swinging back and forth between different models that are all supposed to be the thing that will finally reach the kids for Christ.

You know what will reach the kids for Christ? Sharing Christ with them in the context of a relationship where you and they are fully present. Not distracted or entertained or exhausted by trying to do too much, but really present to listen and talk and share and laugh and cry and do things together.

That's getting harder to do all the time because of our technology. Almost every kid has a smartphone with texting and Facebook, and they carry it everywhere with them. I remember before the Internet took over our lives we could hang out with students for an evening and really get to know them, or have long talks on a bus going to a retreat. Now their heads are down and their thumbs constantly typing a text. We can't disciple anymore because the teenagers' attention spans are too small. They can't hold focus long enough to be discipled because their minds are multitasking at the same bandwidth of their smart phones.

I was talking about this with a friend of mine who works with a nationally known parachurch youth ministry. Here's how he learned to combat this worst element of pop culture.

"Every summer, I take kids up to camp for a week. We rent a large charter bus, and when we get a few hours out from camp, one leader goes around and collects all the kids' cell phones, forcing them to disconnect for a week.

"At first, it's very difficult for them to part with their phones. It became common for kids to try and trick us, bringing an old phone to give to the leader so they could secretly hold on to theirs all week. We didn't try to hide our reasoning from them. We told them we just didn't want them distracted. Lots of them pleaded with us, promising not to text or call as long as they could just have their cell phones on them. One kid actually said to me, 'I can't give it up. I'll feel naked without it.'

"The first day or two is really uncomfortable for them. Some pat their side pockets reaching for phones that are not there, claiming to have felt a vibration. On the way to the first couple meals or activities, the kids talk about these 'phantom vibrations.' The fact that the experience is common to all both entertains and terrifies me at the same time.

"But as these kids disconnect from the distracting outside world, unable to text or check their social media feeds to see what all their friends are up to, the strangest thing happens: they come alive. They engage in the moment and begin to experience all the things they would normally miss out on. Our conversations become richer, and the walls that barricade the vulnerable parts of their souls from being reached come down. Many walk away from the time saying, 'This was the best week of my life!'

"We board the bus at the end of a sleep-deprived, active week and process all the great things that happened. The hours pass, and we get closer and closer to home. One of the leaders begins handing back their phones. The teenagers look at these now foreign devices for a minute or two with confusion. By this point, some remark that they forgot it was gone. But within minutes, headphones go in, texts are sent, and the monotonous silence of virtual reality fills the bus.

"I would never argue that technology is the devil or that the removal of their phones was the only factor contributing to a week of real talks and God encounters. Most of that credit belongs to the Holy Spirit. But I truly believe there is great power in just turning the phones off and being present."

Some churches advocate for embracing the explosion of technology. They want to utilize social media and text messaging as ministry tools. And while there's nothing wrong with that, no amount of status updates, retweets, or Instagram pictures can replace the simple power of an undistracted conversation.

Discipleship is the point of and hope for youth ministry. Evangelism is wonderful, and it is essential for bringing kids into the kingdom of God. But our youth ministries can't be designed to revolve around getting kids to pray a simple "accepting Christ" prayer and then leaving them there. That's only the beginning of their journey with Christ. If we leave them there, they will surely be "...infants, tossed back and forth by the waves, and blown here and there by every wind of teaching and by the cunning and craftiness of people in their deceitful scheming" (Ephesians 4:14). If we leave them at the beginning of their faith and choose not to disciple them, we abandon them as vulnerable babes for that prowling lion–the enemy–to devour.

Go ahead and buy that new shirt and get a cooler pair of glasses if it makes you feel better. But we will never reach the Millennials/GenY by being hipper than they are. They have grown up on a constant diet of mass media. What they need and crave is a person with integrity and truth, who will really listen and genuinely care, someone who will speak into their life the words of eternal life. Let's make that matter to them. Let's show them how relevant Christ can be to them, and how irrelevant pop culture is to the Kingdom.

Chapter 6

The Seduction of Short-Term Missions

A friend of mine recently went on his first overseas missions trip. He was raised in the Church and has supported missions his whole life, but because of jobs and kids and other events in his life, he had never gotten around to actually going on a trip. It was to a small town in Central America that his congregation had been sending teams to for years. Because he had heard the youth pastor and others talk about how great the annual trips were and had seen all the slide shows in the services the week after the teams got back, he had high expectations for what God would do with and through him while he was there. I was curious to hear his impressions after he got back, and while part of me was surprised by what he said, another part of me wasn't.

First of all, he was struck by the poverty that he saw in Central America, but he was also struck by what he didn't see. He said that the physical infrastructure—the roads, the storm drains, the electrical system, the buildings, etc. —was vastly inferior to anything he has seen in the United States, Canada, or in other developed countries. Some streets in this small town in the mountains of Central America were not only dirt: they were deeply rutted and full of potholes. When it rained (which was almost everyday), the drains backed up into the streets. The electricity went out frequently, and the wiring in many of the buildings was exposed and dangerous. The soda pop bottles for sale in the small market looked chipped as if empties had been refilled and resold many times. The local school held some classes outside on old folding chairs under a poorly-built awning. The seats were missing on public toilets, which didn't flush well, and the bathrooms looked like they were not cleaned regularly. Buildings had been left incomplete with stacks of construction materials in the corners of some rooms. What had been built was shoddy. The homes were very small, often just single-room structures of cinder block with makeshift tile or, in a few cases, dirt floors with cheap plastic lawn chairs for furniture.

On the other hand, my friend said that he didn't see anyone who looked hungry. He understands there are places where people don't get enough calories, but this town didn't seem like one of them. The food wasn't as fancy or varied as what we eat here, but there was enough of it, and it was mostly fresh. No one ate highly processed meals from fast food restaurants like too many people here do. The school building wasn't fancy, but the kids took it seriously, walking down the dirt streets in their uniforms and doing homework at night. He couldn't say for sure, but his impression was that the literacy rate wasn't much worse than in America. And his impression was that the people there weren't less happy than people here. Some seemed happy and some didn't, but the ratio wasn't any worse than back in the United States. If anything, his impression of the people in that town was that on average they were happier.

Another thing struck him: almost everyone he met went to some sort of church. Most of them were Roman Catholic, but there was a substantial minority that went to smaller Protestant congregations. There were two Pentecostal congregations in the town, one run by missionaries from America and one that was native.

The missionary church and clinic welcomed their group and put them up in a cinderblock dormitory it kept for American missions groups that came down on a regular basis. Over the next few days, they divided up into two groups to work on different projects. The first group included a few doctors and nurses that saw patients in the local clinic. They diagnosed and treated and performed outpatient surgeries. There were long lines of locals waiting to be seen by the medical missionary staff. The need for their work was obvious.

The second group consisted of young people, youth leaders, and a few adults, of which my friend was one. They went to work doing some light construction. They helped tile a floor in a missionary school. They helped drywall and paint a back room in a church. They helped run electrical to a couple of other buildings and repair a roof. While they worked, they noticed dozens of local men watching them. Some of the locals didn't seem to have much to do during the day. They hung out in front of the market and a small café, drinking coffee. They watched the American high school students carrying materials and painting.

After four days of work and meals with the local church members and worship services in the missionary church in the evenings, they had an excursion day. They all piled into an old, yellow school bus that still had the name of a school district in Texas painted on it. After a two-hour ride down bumpy roads through the mountains, they arrived at a nature preserve. They swam in a pool under a waterfall, hiked to the top of a mountain, and had a wonderful time bonding with God and each other in the natural beauty. The youth pastor led several of the young people to Christ, and others recommitted their lives to serving the Kingdom. Two days later, they were on a plane home.

I asked my friend if he was glad that he had gone on the trip. He assured me that he wouldn't have missed it for the world.

So then I asked him, was it worth it? He paused and thought for a bit. When he answered, he said it depended on what "worth it" meant.

He said that it was worth it for the value it brought to his life. He felt he grew as a Christian and as a person in general through the trip. He learned a lot about another part of the world and another culture. The things he saw impacted his worldview about poverty, our consumer culture, and the American Church's role in the world. It felt good to do hard physical labor for someone out of love without expecting to get paid. Worshipping with people in another culture and language was very moving. Bonding with other team members from his church through these experiences was a spiritual high.

But he said he wasn't sure if it was worth it for the people in the town they visited. The most valuable thing his group had brought to them was the medical team. There were clearly not enough trained doctors and nurses nor enough medicine and equipment in that place. One of the doctors that had come along was an oral surgeon, and he performed some real life-changing operations for several children. A dentist had made a real difference for dozens of patients who had been in pain. A doctor of internal medicine had managed to get a kid sent to the United States to a teaching hospital that donated a highly specialized operation.

On the other hand, he was pretty sure that the group that had spent four days doing light construction and painting brought no value at all. Why were two dozen relatively rich kids from America spending thousands of dollars each to travel to this place and do simple work in front of dozens of local young men standing around with nothing to do all day? Why didn't they paint their own walls? Because they knew that was the job of the groups of American kids that came every few weeks? Because they couldn't afford the paint? Wouldn't it have made more sense to send the cost of one of the group's plane tickets to the local church and have them buy the materials and hire the local men?

And, he wondered, why was it a mission trip? Of course not everyone in that town had a personal, saving relationship with Christ. Many of them went to the local Catholic church out of cultural habit or superstition. But he said that was true back in his city in America. Church attendance in his home town was below fifty percent, and many of those didn't know Christ personally. Why wasn't his city in the United States considered a mission field? And if they were there to spread the Gospel, how were they doing it? They weren't leading people to Christ. How could a bunch of American teenagers that didn't speak Spanish evangelize a town in four days, especially when that town already had at least as many Christians in it as their town back home? Was it because the people there were Hispanic or non-white? The city where he lived was full of immigrants and non-white minorities who lived in poverty, including plenty of Hispanics. Why wasn't his church putting time and effort and money into reaching those people who were only a few miles away?

My friend captured many of my feelings about short-term mission trips, especially for students. They make a big difference in the lives of the kids who go.

They are amazing opportunities for spiritual growth, for bonding a group, and for inspiring a young person to take their walk with Christ and responsibilities in God's Kingdom more seriously.

God does great things in the lives of many students while on a short-term mission trip. For this reason, I highly recommend that students consider going on one if they can.

However, I have some real concerns. We promote them as "mission" trips, whose purpose is to enlarge God's Kingdom on the mission field. But all the benefits I mentioned in the last paragraph relate to enlarging God's Kingdom in the hearts of the students. In that sense, their greatest value is as discipleship or educational retreats. But that's not how we "sell" them when we are fundraising for our youth groups. Our congregations care about the Great Commission, and it's easier to get support for these trips than for basic discipleship or evangelism of the unchurched kids in our hometown.

Some youth pastors are seduced by all the excitement around short-term missions. They spend a lot of time planning, promoting, raising money for, or recuperating from short term mission trips. They justify all that time, money, and energy not by explaining that these are educational retreats but that we are off to some developing country to save the lost.

In some churches, the emphasis on short-term mission trips have grown out of proportion to their value to the kids or the people on the mission field. Meanwhile, the "lower hanging fruit" of outreach to our cities and within our kids has been overlooked. I'm not saying students shouldn't go on these trips at all, but I am saying that if our purpose is discipleship of our students, then we could do more to disciple them than spending thousands of dollars to fly them somewhere for a week. What are we doing to grow Christ in them the other fifty-one weeks a year? If we pursued discipleship more year-round, would these trips be as necessary?

And if we care about teaching our kids to do evangelism, why do we need to take them thousands of miles away? There are probably non-white minority kids, including immigrants who speak another language, within a few miles of our churches. Why don't we invest in those outreach efforts more consistently? We might grow our kids, grow our congregations, and grow the Kingdom without having to spend half of the year planning for a mission trip, preparing for a mission trip, or recovering from a mission trip.

Chapter 7

Who Has the Youth Pastor's Back?

Let's be real honest about something: youth ministry is a job.

Yes, it's a calling from the Lord. Yes, it's a vocation. Yes, it can and should be a holy pursuit, an act of Christlike servanthood. It is all those things.

But there is a human aspect to it as well. A youth pastor has a position with responsibilities he or she must fulfill. There is someone, sometimes more than one, who holds them accountable for fulfilling those responsibilities. If it is a paid position, there are expectations (not always clearly expressed) for how those responsibilities should be carried out and how "success" will be measured. And like a lot of jobs that involve leading groups of people, there are pressures and politics. Expectations and demands come from multiple directions; different groups or stakeholders within the congregation often want different things. It isn't an easy job. In addition to discerning how God is leading and what the kids need, a youth pastor has to figure out how to operate in an organization with hundreds or even thousands of members, all of whom have an opinion about the youth ministry and how it's going. The youth pastor is often caught in the middle of a political landscape he or she doesn't understand. And far too often, the youth pastor is a young adult without the career experience to navigate through it all.

And so, youth pastors usually need someone who "has their back." They need someone who will help them to receive, understand, and cope with criticism. Sometimes, they need someone who will deflect criticism so they can concentrate on their work. They need someone who will help them request and get the resources they need from a church budget that is usually strained. They need someone to help them grow professionally and develop into a seasoned staff person. They need someone to encourage them when they are struggling, to tell them when they are wrong, and even to help them know when it's time to move on to a new ministry.

But too many youth pastors never find anyone to professionally mentor and protect them within the congregation. Many hope the senior pastor will fill that role, but it's not uncommon for there to be a twenty-five year age difference between a senior pastor and a youth pastor. Not only are they in different stages in life, they have very different roles within the church. They often have very different expectations from the relationship. The youth pastor might long for the senior pastor to be a mentor and coach, while the senior pastor needs a competent employee to run the youth program without problems or controversy.

After my friend Tom was hired as a youth pastor, he met with his senior pastor. They talked about an "open door policy" that would allow Tom talk to his boss any time he wanted. But as Tom settled into his job, it became clear that this pastor only met with staff individually if it was absolutely necessary—and as he found out, the senior pastor would decide when it was "absolutely necessary."

Actually, the senior pastor was only the big boss. Tom's immediate supervisor was another staff member. Shortly after Tom moved into his office, he ran into some minor problems and misunderstandings about the youth program. He went to his new supervisor and sought advice. He laid out a few dilemmas—how could he keep various groups and individuals happy when they all expected different things? Tom was hoping for a wise mentor, someone who would coach him through rough patches as he developed his ministry career. His supervisor listened and told Tom that he would have to figure those things out for himself. Tom was confused: wasn't that what the staff was there to help him do? Then his supervisor explained how things actually worked within the congregation. "Sink or swim," his supervisor said, "you're on your own."

"In retrospect," Tom said, "I should have called for a meeting of the personnel committee that week and resigned. But at the ripe age of twenty-five, I didn't know that. As it was, I served there four years, grinding out ministry through ongoing private criticism and finally a lengthy evaluation process that lasted nine months. After four months, it dawned on me that he [the supervisor] (and by then a few others) wanted me to resign. While students' lives were being changed and the youth group grew, all sorts of things were being criticized. I endured it because I wanted to learn from it.

"I was told that a five-person personnel committee had questioned my teaching abilities. Then, I heard that they had sat in my sessions and determined I was a good teacher after all. This personnel committee then questioned my marriage and sent a representative to my house, only to later 'approve' of my marriage. Then, this group questioned my leadership abilities, only to later say they were fine. They kept looking for some reason to get rid of me, and then changing their mind.

"The weird thing was, I had never met with them. In staff meetings or from my supervisor I would hear negative feedback like, 'You're just not a good fit for this team,' or, 'We really like who you are but not the general direction of the youth ministry,' or, 'Youth ministry probably isn't your calling; have you thought about going back to school?' I realized I needed to run and not look back.

"It's good I came to that conclusion, because eventually I was called before this personnel committee. They told me the coming Sunday would be my last. I was to resign at the council meeting in three days and then attend church for the last time in six days.

"At the council meeting, when it was my turn on the agenda, I addressed the twelve people in the room and told them I would willingly leave the position since they had asked me to. I would, of course, submit to their leadership and leave without causing problems, but I could not resign myself. I could not look students in the eye and tell them this was my idea. The Personnel Committee Chair said, 'We won't give you a severance package unless you do this our way.' But the seven other elders looked shocked and expressed that they were told it was my idea to resign. They didn't know I had been asked to leave.

"I left the room, and they had quite a long discussion. Later, I was told they would honor the severance package I was offered. Several elders called me to express their appreciation for my work and my humility."

The Senior Pastor was missing altogether in this equation. Originally, he had talked to Tom about an open door policy to his office, but that's not how he ran things in reality. It seemed this senior pastor valued plausible deniability—he could say that he wasn't personally involved in the controversy. Tom said, "No one supervised my supervisor, and no one on the personnel committee offered to meet with me or meet in an ongoing way."

Tom's ministry crumbled beneath him partially because the senior pastor failed to build a relationship in which he could watch over and disciple this younger pastor. Too often, senior pastors treat youth workers as junior employees, allowed to function independently unless something goes wrong. In very large congregations with big staffs, the youth pastor might very well be two or three levels below the senior pastor on the organizational chart. But without a mentor, coach, or patron—much less a protector—a young youth pastor is going to fail.

Most senior pastors don't want the youth pastor to fail and aren't intentionally neglectful. They have huge responsibilities of their own and not enough hours in their week to mentor the entire staff. But if they can't watch the youth pastor's back, who will?

Have they created a staff culture that allows a young staff person to grow and even to make mistakes along the way?

If the senior pastor can't or won't work to initiate a nurturing culture, who will? It certainly can't come from the bottom up: the leader has to lead. And if a senior pastor won't pastor his own staff, won't invest in their development, who will? I understand how much pressure they are under and how hard their jobs are. But I have seen far too many youth pastors fail and youth ministries struggle because of senior pastors who wouldn't take responsibility for helping them to succeed. Ultimately, the kids suffer as their program is impacted by the revolving door of youth pastors. All these junior staffers take the heat, but the buck has to stop at the desk of the senior leader. If he doesn't have the time to personally take a youth pastor under his wing, then it's his job to manage his team so that someone does. Great preachers are not always great managers. The one thing that should never happen, and sadly does too often, is for the youth pastor to be the designated scapegoat for a senior pastor's mismanagement of his organization.

In my first youth ministry, I served with a pastor who was a great man. He was a teacher, mentor, and a believer in people and their gifts. As I served him and the church, we built up a good relationship, and he would guide me through rough situations. The first challenge I encountered with that pastor came in my third month of employment. In May of 1986, I got a call at about 3 a.m. from a young lady in our youth group. Her grandfather had just died, and she wanted me to come visit her home. I called the senior pastor, passed on the news, but went back to bed.

When I got to work the next morning, he called me in his office and began to ask me why I was in ministry. He said that he was disappointed in my decision not to go to the young lady's house and minister to her and her family. That day I learned a valuable lesson: get up, get out, and reach people one person or one situation at a time. It was a principle that I have never forgotten. From that day on, I developed a strong relationship with my senior pastor.

He not only released me to do ministry, he also guided me through its opportunities and challenges one day at a time.

This senior pastor took the time to build a relationship with me, and because our work together was rooted in that relationship, we were able to trust each other and grow together. Because we were a team, God blessed other projects we tackled together.

During my service at that church, an opportunity arose for me to help coach a local high school men's soccer team. It would be an assistant position where I would work with the team from 3:30 p.m. to 5:30 p.m. almost every weekday. I approached the senior pastor and told him about the opportunity. I explained why I thought it would help me to be more effective in the community, investing in area students and inviting them into our youth ministry. The conversation didn't take long. He saw the value in the opportunity and said, "Go for it." The coaching gig turned into a nine year position. It eventually opened another door for me to become the head coach for the women's soccer team. Largely because we stepped through these open doors, our youth ministry grew from twenty-six students to over 350 in just a few years.

What a joy it was to serve with a senior pastor like this man! Because he took the time to know my heart and establish a relationship, he was able to both discipline me and give me his blessing to pursue opportunities like the soccer coaching. He wasn't intimidated by the growth of the youth program. In fact, he embraced my ideas about reaching the next generation and helped me to do whatever it took to bring students through the door so we could win them for Christ and disciple them to maturity.

Every youth pastor deserves a senior leader like I had at that church. Every senior pastor needs to manage his staff in such a way that a young youth pastor has opportunities to grow and even to make mistakes. But if we want to make youth ministry in America really matter for the next generation, youth pastors will need to take risks for Christ. They can only do that if someone has their back.

Chapter 8

Why Youth Pastors and Senior Staff Need Each Other

In chapter seven, I explain why a youth pastor needs his senior pastor to provide coaching, support, and sometimes even protection. Far too often, youth pastors are forced to navigate the congregation's complex expectations and politics by themselves. The senior pastor leaves them to sink or swim alone. For a youth pastor in his or her early twenties, often in their first ministry job, this can be a confusing and frustrating adventure that, too often, ends badly.

But why? How come so many (not all, of course) senior pastors either neglect (at best) or actively undermine the youth pastor? What possible motivation could they have for allowing or even causing a junior staff member, ministering to students, to fail? How could that possibly be a good thing? How could it benefit a senior pastor?

To answer that question, let me tell you a story about a youth pastor I'll call "Brad."

Brad took a job as a youth pastor while he was in seminary. The church was small and located in a semi-rural suburb about half an hour outside of a medium-sized city in the Midwest. There were about thirty senior high students, and almost all of them had grown up in the congregation together. But as they moved into their teenage years, they became bored with the very traditional Sunday services and sermons. They weren't really rebellious as much as they were disengaged.

The previous youth pastor had run the senior high youth nights using a denominational curriculum. It was very structured and basically amounted to Sunday school for sixteen year-olds. The kids came because their parents made them come and because there wasn't much else to do on Wednesday nights in their sleepy little town. When Brad started, he did away with the dull curriculum, and he organized the youth nights around an informal worship service. A couple of the students played guitars and led the group through a few praise and worship songs, Brad gave a short Bible message, and then they broke up into small groups for discussion and prayer. Brad was engaging and empathetic and set a model for faith that the kids could understand and follow. In six months, it transformed the group. The kids felt there was finally a place in the congregation where they could worship and engage with God and where they would be taken seriously. A few began to invite friends and stragglers returned. Although the group didn't explode in size, the senior high group added perhaps a dozen new members. Considering the size of the congregation, this was considered a great success.

Beyond the numbers, the parents were thrilled with Brad's ministry. Their kids now wanted to go to youth group without being nagged. The students were more enthusiastic and vocal about their faith and more willing to pitch in for service projects and volunteer duties, like working in the nursery on Sundays. The parents thought Brad was the best thing that had happened in that church for their sons and daughters in years.

There was a tradition in this congregation: one Sunday morning every spring, the senior high students were allowed to take over and lead a worship service for the full congregation. The annual "youth service" let the students pick songs, play instruments, lead the announcements, and take a special offering for their summer mission trip.

The youth pastor was allowed to give the message. Most years, the kids just went through the motions. They were usually scared to be in front of the congregation and forced to use songs and a program they weren't enthusiastic about. But this year would be different. Brad had been there almost a year, and this was the first congregational youth service they had led since they started their new format on Wednesday night. Over the previous six months, they had gotten more practice being in front of a room and leading worship. They wanted to lead the congregation with the praise songs that they used in their own group instead of hymns from pew hymnals like every other Sunday morning. And they were excited and proud to have Brad, the youth pastor they had come to love, preach a message to the full congregation for the first time.

The service was a huge success. The students worked hard to prepare, and it showed. Their enthusiasm was contagious, and the older members of the congregation, including many of their grandparents, were thrilled to see the young people praising God and leading with maturity. It felt like an infusion of energy and creativity into a pattern of worship that had become a little stale and familiar. And Brad's message, while it wouldn't have won any awards, was delivered with freshness and sincerity. Almost the entire congregation was grateful for and proud of what he had done with their students. That year's annual youth service was an acknowledgment that another generation was growing up and would eventually carry the congregation into the future.

During the coffee and fellowship time afterward, Brad's hand got shaken and his back slapped over and over as parents and grandparents thanked him for what he had done with the young people. Some folks, including a few members of the church board, told him that it had been a breath of fresh air and that they would like to sing some of those songs more often. Brad and the young people high-fived each other. It was a great day.

Two days later, the senior pastor invited Brad to meet him for lunch. When he got to the restaurant, the chairman of the elders was waiting in a booth next to the senior pastor. The two older men greeted him warmly and made small talk while they ordered. Once the waitress left with the menus, the senior pastor cleared his throat and told Brad that "concerns" had been "expressed" at the elders' meeting the evening before.

He went on to tell Brad that "a number" of people were concerned that the youth group needed more "structure" and "discipline." There were also concerns that the youth ministry's content had become too "light" and not "biblically-based."

The elders wanted to be sure that the young people were being fed "solid food" and not "spiritual candy."

The elders had asked the senior pastor (Brad later found that it was the other way around) to take a more active role overseeing and mentoring Brad. Brad would submit all of his youth group lesson plans in writing, including songs and his messages, to the senior pastor at least two weeks in advance. The senior pastor would edit and approve Brad's plans and messages with a red pen. To preserve staff unity, Brad was not to tell anyone else about this arrangement. If the senior pastor vetoed or changed any songs, message topics, or program ideas Brad was to tell the senior high leadership team that he, Brad, had changed his mind. He was to use his popularity with the students and parents to "sell" these changes.

Brad was flabbergasted, and stared in disbelief when the food arrived. Hadn't the youth service, just a few days before, been a huge success? When he asked that question, he was told that it was not his place as a youth pastor to create expectations for changes in the congregation's worship style. All of the sudden, it became clear to Brad: the success of the youth service had put some pressure on the senior pastor to introduce contemporary elements into the worship services on a more regular basis. And Brad's popularity with the kids, as well as their parents and grandparents, was threatening to the senior pastor. But why? He was just a seminary student. There was no way he was going to take the senior pastor's job away, unless...unless the senior pastor was a deeply insecure man.

Brad's pastor saw him, and the changes he was introducing through the youth program as a threat to his own control. He didn't like and wasn't experienced in contemporary worship and preaching. If too many people pushed to move the worship style in that direction, it might make him look inadequate. He couldn't effectively lead a contemporary church, and he knew it. His base of support was the traditionalists within the congregation.

And so he convinced the elders to let him squelch the expectations that Brad was creating with his ministry.

Insecurity is often at the root of senior vs. youth pastor conflict. By the nature of their position, many youth pastors are popular within the congregation. Young people and their parents love and appreciate them. Adult volunteers in the youth program accompany them on youth retreats and mission trips. They lead neighborhood kids to Christ and oversee fun events like car washes and carnivals. What's not to love? If a youth pastor runs an effective program and is likable, he can easily become a favorite staff member in many people's eyes.

And sadly, many senior pastors feel very insecure in their positions. They worry about building programs and budgets. They have to hire and fire and make some tough decisions. Many know that they have political opponents in the congregation. And sometimes they look with envy on the winsome and lovable youth pastor.

I've seen this over and over. In addition to Brad, I could tell you "Dean's" story. Dean was a youth pastor in a contemporary church of about four thousand members. He organized a city-wide outreach that introduced positive changes in poor neighborhoods with students from broken homes. He recruited senior high students who had grown up in stable Christian families to mentor troubled kids. He got students involved in food pantry and tutoring programs. He held some large outreach concerts in which some gang members came forward, gave their lives to Christ, and turned over their guns. Because of his successes, several local newspapers ran articles and a local television station did a short news piece about him one night. The morning after he was on the local news, Dean walked into the conference room for the weekly staff meeting. The other staff, standing around and waiting for everyone else to arrive, began teasing him. They asked if he had his resume updated and printed. Dean was confused; why would he need his resume? The other staff explained that the senior pastor would never tolerate another staff member getting more attention in the media than he did.

"Kirk" had a similar experience as a senior high youth pastor at a megachurch with a prominent television ministry. The senior pastor was a star in the evangelical world with a weekly television show that was broadcast internationally. When Kirk wrote a book about youth ministry that began to get national attention, he found out how insecure a television star can be. Standing in the parking lot, talking to some friends, he saw the pastor's luxury car pull over and the tinted window roll down. He was waved over. The senior pastor didn't even get out of the car to tell him that he should stop giving interviews to magazines about his book. The focus of any media attention needed to be the church's weekly services, featuring the senior pastor's preaching, and broadcast around the globe.

It doesn't have to be this way.

Senior pastors and youth pastors need each other.

They serve very different needs within the congregation, and if both succeed, the congregation will only be stronger. Both need to learn to forge a bond, which helps the other. The senior pastor's ministry can only become more effective if students are reached and retained in the congregation. The youth pastor, no matter how popular, poses no real threat to the senior leader. I have never heard of a congregation replacing the senior pastor with a youth minister. On the other hand, the youth minister needs to recognize that the senior pastor's job is to lead the whole congregation, and so he sees a bigger picture. The senior pastor can help the youth pastor to put student ministries in perspective and to support them financially. That might require the youth pastor to release some of his or her own insecurities or to be teachable and patient.

Brad resigned rather than submit his plans for review. As it was presented to him, I'm not sure I blame him. But what if he had tried to engage the senior pastor and the elders earlier in the process? What if he had a better grasp of how important traditional worship was to many people in the congregation and had found ways to prepare them for the youth service in advance? We'll never know what would have happened, but my hope and prayer is that senior and youth pastors would find ways to come together and serve each other as they together serve Christ. If they can model that kind of teamwork, our churches would be healthier and the generations less divided—and church staffs would not be fractured by ongoing conflict and rotating junior staff members. In the end, everyone will win.

Chapter 9

It Takes a Village: Why the Congregation Needs to Get Involved

Matt realized that his youth ministry was succeeding when guns started showing up at church. But convincing the adult members and elders of that was another matter.

Matt was a youth pastor at a medium-sized church in a large metro area. The church wasn't "urban," but it was located in the transition zone between the rough parts of the city and the suburbs. The members tended to be from the suburban "side of the tracks," although in recent years more families from neighborhoods plagued by crime and gangs began attending worship services and other programs. The church's campus consisted of half a city block, most of which was parking, with a main worship center and two or three annex buildings for classrooms and offices. The youth center consisted of a basketball gymnasium/multipurpose room with a couple of classroom-sized spaces attached to it. Along the far side of the parking lot, where a residential block began, the church had bought several homes for key staff members to live in.

Although they weren't architecturally special, the congregation was proud of its facilities and worked hard to maintain them. They fought a battle to keep their campus clean and safe. The custodian was constantly painting over graffiti "tags" on walls and calling the police when strange cars pulled into the lot after midnight, usually for drug deals. In fact, for several years, drug dealing had been creeping from the inner city into this transitional community. The police had actually used the church's parking lot as a staging area for drug raids on crack houses a mile away. The church offices had been burglarized several times with computers and petty cash stolen. Some members of the church felt that their congregation was a fortress in an increasingly hostile territory. They welcomed anyone to visit their services or midweek programs, but they wanted their church to remain peaceful and wholesome.

Matt didn't want trouble, but his heart broke for the kids who were growing up in neighborhoods—just a few blocks away—where drugs, gangs, and crime were just a way of life. Could his youth ministry ignore them? Could his church really be an authentic witness to God's Kingdom if the community saw it as a fortress? Why was he taking students on an annual mission trip overseas, at a cost of thousands of dollars per student, when there was a mission field a mile away?

Matt concluded that for his youth ministry to be an extension of God's love for the local kids who didn't know Christ, he had to find a way to engage them in his program.

His senior pastor had a heart for the city and agreed with Matt's vision. He promised to do everything he could to support Matt's outreach to the area, regardless of who that brought onto the campus. With that blessing, Matt began to turn the youth ministry into a more evangelistic program to engage the teenagers who never came to church and were falling into the drug and gang culture.

His methods weren't particularly innovative, just well-executed and effective. He adjusted the Wednesday night program to be more of an evangelistic rally. He tweaked the musical style a bit to make it more appealing to the teenagers he was targeting without compromising the integrity of the worship. He put up flyers around town and gave everyone he knew a stack of business cards with the name of the group, the time of the youth service, directions, and told them to pass them out to all the kids they met. He talked to police and juvenile corrections officers that were Christians and told them about what he was doing so that they could suggest the youth service to teenagers who might be interested. He started a separate small-group discipleship program to minister to the Christian students that had been in the church for years and used those students as leaders for the Wednesday night rallies.

It worked. Not overnight, but over a couple of years, attendance at the Wednesday night youth service went from seventy-five students to three hundred. Most of the growth came from the very kids Matt was targeting, those who lived in rough neighborhoods with broken families and were falling into a life of drugs, gangs, and much worse.

The first time guns showed up, everyone freaked out. A teen who had come to several rallies invited a few of his friends. Three of them showed up one Wednesday night in a car outfitted and painted in the style that was popular with local gangs at the time. They wore gang-style clothes although they didn't display any gang "colors." The three of them caused no trouble and seemed engaged in the music and the message. But near the end of the evening another student saw a pistol tucked into one of the visitor's waistband under his baggy shirt. The girl who saw it was frightened, and she reported it to an adult leader, who panicked and called Matt over. Matt calmed everyone down and told the visitor that he was welcome to come participate but that weapons and drugs were absolutely not allowed on the campus.

A few weeks later, someone saw a gun in a visitor's car in the parking lot after the rally. A week or so after that, a verbal shouting match in the parking lot after the Wednesday night youth service led to some threats and a gun being flashed by a visitor. No one had gotten hurt in any of these incidents, but the adult leaders and many of the staff worried that it was just a matter of time before someone did. If gang members were showing up, the odds of a conflict were growing. The staff and the church elders held a meeting to address the issue.

At the meeting, Matt explained why he felt that the guns were a sign that the youth ministry was succeeding in engaging the community where they lived. Of course, he didn't welcome the guns themselves, but the teens that lived in that culture were coming to the youth rallies, and many of them were starting to follow Jesus. A number were working hard to change their lives and escape the problems that the guns symbolized.

His senior pastor backed him up, just as he had promised. In fact, over the last year the senior pastor had allowed a young man, who had come to Christ and was trying to leave the gang life behind, to live in his home. The senior pastor lived in one of the houses the church owned on the edge of its property. This nineteen-year-old young man had been converted through Matt's youth ministry and other programs in the church. He was making a sincere effort to change and needed to get out of the environment where he had been living for many years. The senior pastor and his wife felt led by the Lord to offer to let him stay in a little guest room that had been built over their garage. They found him a local job and a school program where he could work on his G.E.D. (high school equivalency program). Matt knew that the senior pastor didn't just talk the talk, he walked the walk.

The senior pastor convinced the elders and the staff that they all needed to support the youth ministry's evangelistic outreach. Obviously, they didn't want any violence or criminal activity on their campus. But they couldn't discourage these youth from visiting the Wednesday night services and hearing the gospel. The senior pastor suggested that the entire congregation would have to work together to make the program work while preserving their campus, the congregation's values, and everyone's safety.

First, they needed security that would keep everyone safe. The senior pastor asked for, and got, a budget to hire off-duty police officers to be on campus during youth nights. They wanted some of them to be visible, to discourage the brandishing of weapons or conflict between rival gangs. A few police were in plain clothes, just to keep moving around campus and to stand in the back of the youth service, providing an extra layer of safety. There were a few other security measures put in place to preserve the property. Overall, security ended up being a significant expense in the youth budget. But with the senior pastor's help, the congregation came to accept this as the cost of fulfilling their mission in the community.

Second, they realized that it wasn't enough to just lead teens through the Sinner's Prayer. They had to have programs in place to help these young people to grow in Christ. That meant Bible studies, but it also meant much more. The congregation increased its food bank and other benevolence measures so that the families of these young people would have some support as they tried to change their lives. A number of older people volunteered to help with tutoring and mentoring, so young people who came to faith through the youth ministry could stay in school and work through other issues in their life.

Third, the congregation supported additional youth ministry staff and facilities to accommodate the growth. This meant that resources were redirected from some other programs and projects. Members could have objected, but they realized that their congregation had an opportunity to make an impact in the community through outreach to these young people. Adults who weren't directly involved in the youth ministry felt that they could contribute to the mission by adjusting their programs and helping with facility expansion.

What Matt accomplished was not unique; other youth programs around the country have impacted their communities in similar ways.

What was unique was how the congregation embraced the growth and overcame the challenges.

Far too often, these kinds of changes cause conflict between youth and adult ministries and result in the youth pastor being reeled in or let go. But Matt's senior pastor saw the opportunity to expand the Kingdom through the youth ministry and led the congregation to support it at many levels. There is an old saying: it takes a village to raise a child. I say that in many of our cities today, it takes the entire congregation to reach a generation falling further away from Christ. As more teenagers in America grow up without an intact family, congregations have an opportunity to make their church a welcoming home for kids who need to meet Jesus.

Chapter 10

There Are People Doing it Right

One of the problems about writing a critique about anything is that readers might misunderstand and believe that you have a negative perspective. For the record, I think that we have challenges as youth pastors in America today, but I don't think that the news is all bad or that we can't rise up and overcome those challenges. There are youth pastors out there who are doing it right. There are leaders who are helping teenagers become relevant to God's Kingdom rather than watering down the Gospel to shoehorn it into popular culture. There are some great youth pastors who are making it matter.

One of them is my friend, Eran Holt. Eran is the student ministry pastor at Real Life Student Ministries, which is the youth department of Glad Tidings Church in Reading, Pennsylvania. Eran is like me: neither of us is a short-term youth pastor, only working in student ministries for a couple of years so we can move on to something we want to do more. Eran has been in his current position for eleven and-a-half years. I respect his commitment to the Gospel, to the students, and to reaching them the right way. Here's how he described his ministry.

"The youth ministry I grew up in had a relatively simple process for mentoring students: Salvation, Discipleship, Ministry Involvement, and then Student Leadership. Several years ago, in our current youth ministry, we recognized a major shift in today's generation and how they received the mentoring process. We began to question our process for mentoring students and ultimately raising them up to serve as student leaders in our ministry. We discovered that this generation of students values ownership and opportunity to serve at such a level that, if they are kept at arm's length until they've grown spiritually through salvation and discipleship, they often times won't be around long enough for us to develop a relationship with them and thus be able to have a mentoring role in their life.

"That said, we've reversed the process. Student leadership is now defined as serving as a ministry volunteer anywhere in our church. We've moved away from a more traditional model of student leadership, which is typically a handful of students that are leaders just in the context of one's youth ministry. This model alienates the dozens of students in our churches that love to serve in children's ministry, media ministry, worship ministry, and students in the church who don't go to your youth ministry but will still serve somewhere. We want to value any student who is serving anywhere in our church, regardless of their attendance at our youth ministry.

"The logistics of our model are broken down like this:

- When a student wants to serve in ministry they fill out a short application with our Serve Team. This is the team of volunteers that handle all students and adults in the church that are looking for serving opportunities.
- A coach from the Serve ministry will help place a student in a ministry serving role that provides a good fit for their passions, gifts, and interest.
- The student is now serving in ministry and thus considered a student leader in our church and youth ministry. Here's where the mentoring process begins.
- Four to six times a year, the student ministry hosts student leader events, training sessions, field trips, etc.

to provide discipleship and leadership-orientated training opportunities for our students. We partner with various other departments in our church in hosting these events, especially the departments that have a larger number of student volunteers, like our children's ministry. Our events will be as large a day trip to historical locations to study leadership or as small as a meal with a short lesson on leadership.

"With this model, we have been able to accomplish the following: We are encouraging students to serve where their hearts lead them as opposed to forcing them to fit into the model of serving just in the student ministry.

- We are discipling students and training them to be leaders after they are serving, which makes their hearts become more open as the material is more relevant to their spiritual journey.
- We are building relationships with our students during our training events, which is especially important for the students that are serving in ministry in our church but haven't really connected very well with our youth ministry. Our model allows us to reach those students and affirms their serving in ministry.

- We are mentoring and building up a generation of leaders who have learned the importance of serving. It's a culture that every student ministry needs to have."

Eran describes a key component to truly effective discipleship for anyone of any age: getting them to serve others as soon as possible. If the goal of discipleship—of the Christian life in general—is to reproduce Jesus' heart and character in his followers, then serving is not just an end, but it is a means to get there.

We don't serve because we have become like Christ; we become like Christ because we serve other people like He did.

To be a follower of someone means following in his footsteps, in same way that he walked. Servanthood isn't the destination; it's the path.

Through his ministry, Eran has learned that students can't be passive. Our goal in youth ministry can't be entertainment, education, discipleship, and then service.

Our goal is to get kids following Jesus as soon as possible by living like Jesus. That means letting go of selfishness and giving to others. By finding ways to get kids serving in their area of passion as early in their Christian life as possible, they are learning the way of the Gospel from the inside out.

This is the crux of the difference between the "relevant" models and the "irRelevant" model I propose. The culturally relevant model treats students as consumers to be catered to by bringing the Kingdom to their level.

The Kingdom relevant model (irRelevant) raises students up from their culture so they can become more like Jesus and useful to his Kingdom.

All that sounds theoretical, but Eran has found a practical way to incorporate that into his program by recruiting the youth to serve in the area of their gifts and passions as soon as possible.

A lot of youth pastors are doing it right. They understand that youth ministry is a lifetime calling, not a stepping stone. These pastors aren't in it "until I grow up" or "until something better comes along." They see before them a lost and dying generation, a mission field of American teenagers that desperately needs to know Jesus Christ. Sharing the Gospel with children and youth has become the greatest calling in their lives. We should recognize them because reaching the next generation around us is one of the greatest callings upon the Church in America today.

The people who are doing it right have a Kingdom vision. They go beyond just being a youth leader. They take on the roles of mentor, teacher, educator, and life-giver as well. They see how this culture pulls down people who lack a firm spiritual foundation, and they are committed to helping young people build that foundation as soon as possible. These youth leaders don't just talk the talk of reaching the next generation, they walk the walk. They recognize that there is power in both the talk (the Bible reminds us over and over that the tongue has the power to build or destroy lives), but they also remember the Word saying: "The kingdom of God is not a matter of talk but of power" (1 Corinthians 4:20). God wants more than just words.

The youth pastors who are doing it right know that they are. They realize that God has placed a special call in their lives. They don't shrink from that call; they embrace it. They have discovered, accepted, and developed their gifts. They don't hide behind the crutch of programs (the ones that aren't working) that just go through the motions, counting students and moving them through an assembly line like widgets in a factory. They are really entering into the lives of these young people and cultivating God's unique gifts in each student. There is passion and life in what they do.

The youth pastors that are doing it right also value their staff. They care about and recognize the gifts of the team that they've assembled. They deeply invest in their staff, and they work alongside them to make the whole group more effective.

There is a flip side to this, however. Unfortunately, there are people in youth ministry who *weren't* called. Some are doing youth ministry because they grew up in a church where it was expected of them or because a pastor persuaded them to take it on, despite having no real gifts or passion. They might be conscientious and work hard at it, but there is no real anointing of the Spirit to their ministry because there was no real call. They feel no joy in doing it either. Youth pastors that are genuinely called understand and accept that they have a divine appointment or mandate from God to reach teenagers. That call anoints their life. They don't worry about financial packages or benefits before accepting it. They make themselves available to the Kingdom and trust that God will provide as they step out in faith.

Corey Ten Boom, Mother Teresa, and Reinhard Bonnke all made enormous differences for Christ. They are heroes of the faith. But ordinary people can and are making those kinds of differences today regardless of recognition or fame. They are doing it in youth ministries that are helping the next generation to step up and be relevant to God's Kingdom.

I have been privileged enough to see little glimpses of this through others in my own youth ministry journey. I saw it through my friend, Shawn, who I watched take the time after church to walk a young lady through a horrible situation where her mother died. I saw it in a Eran, who embraced a young man, verbally abused by his family, and empowered him to become a leader in ministry. I saw it in my friend, Lee, who directed and guided young people to effectively win their school campuses to Christ. Each of these youth pastors, ordinary people on the field, took young people that Jesus called "the least of these" and helped them become relevant and useful to the cause of Christ.

And it's not just youth pastors. Senior pastors are investing in these youth pastors to build them up in Christ. My own mentor, Robert G. Muirhead, took this raw twenty-six year-old and said, "You're my youth pastor." He had coffee with me every day, investing in me and pouring wisdom and guidance into my life. These true mentors, like my Grandpap, want to bestow gifts and raise up the next leaders to be better than they were.

There are kids that are doing it right, too. Seventeen year-old Jonathan Pierce, known by all his friends as JP, was a high school junior that just died of cancer. This kid understood when he was diagnosed at fifteen that he was a missionary in a mission field called "high school." That kid died walking into the kingdom of God. JP made a huge difference where he was at, and I'd argue that he understood what *calling* entailed better than most. I know kids in my ministry in Michigan, right now, who make breakfast and dinner for their own moms and dads—who are more mature and responsible than their own parents. These kids know that Christ is their only hope, but that they are called to love and serve those around them, just like Jesus.

Youth pastors who are in it for the long haul are the people doing it right.

They are the ones not worried about accolades. They acknowledge that short-term missions are important, but they also know the power of walking across the street in order to be an effective tool for the Kingdom. Their motives lie in serving the King, not in impressing others or being persuaded by other people's opinions. A pat on the back is six inches from a stab in the back. The people doing it right don't work for man; they work for Christ. They persevere through the storms and choose to surrender everything to Christ, despite their failures and short-comings.

That is how you do it right. That is how you make it matter. That is how we make youth ministry irRelevant.

Chapter 11

Fathers and Mothers

We all look forward to hearing our Father in heaven say, "Well done." But many of us have never heard that from our fathers and mothers on earth and desperately wished that we had.

And over my career in youth ministry, I have tried to bless kids that no one else has. But no youth pastor—no matter how gifted or committed—can replace a parent. Parents have a unique role in our life, a special job that only they can do.

That is especially true for fathers. I have come to believe that one of the biggest problems our nation faces is the millions of kids growing up without a father playing an active role in their life. There are all sorts of reasons why dads are disappearing, but the bottom line is that they are. A generation that doesn't know a Godly father on earth will have a hard time understanding their Father in

Heaven. If fathers do not invest in their children's lives, it leaves a hole that only God's grace can fill.

In my first ministry, I met a young man (let's call him David) who was very confused about his identity. His parents never married, and his father was sent to prison for a number of felonies before David was born. David's mother and grandparents did the best they could to teach him right from wrong. They started bringing him to church when he was little. They made sure he went to Sunday school and other kids' programs and eventually the junior high youth ministry. But by the time he was thirteen, David was angry and distraught and becoming mean and violent. He started fights, bullied other kids, and began to steal.

David was in and out of our ministry, and his mother continued to ask for our help with him. I hate to admit it, but there were weeks we would hope and pray that he wouldn't show up because he was so disruptive. We couldn't give other kids the attention they needed. His mom knew her son was out of control, and she was desperate for someone to invest in him. We did the best we could to help raise David, but he ran with the wrong crowd and wouldn't let anyone who might have been a positive influence get close to him. By the age of fifteen, he found himself in and out of juvenile homes. School wasn't for learning; it was just a place where he got in trouble. He didn't recognize or respect any authority figures in his life.

I remember getting a call one time because David had gotten into some trouble. When I showed up, he got mad at me. He thought the whole world was against him. It didn't matter that people like myself and a few others would come and try to walk him through difficult times. He hated the fact that when he needed help, his father didn't come. He longed for the love that only a father could give.

One night, he showed up to the youth ministry very distraught. He had gotten into a fight at school that day and was taken off the school property. That evening, the youth group was having a back-to-school outreach. More than a hundred kids showed up, and everyone was having a great time. David began acting like a bully, provoking conflicts. It wasn't long before he was picking a fight with some of the other boys. I had no choice but to pull him aside and regain control of the situation. David hated that and challenged me and my authority. As much as I cared about David, I had a responsibility to let the other hundred kids have a positive experience. I had some of the other leaders take him aside and try and talk through his problems, but it made no difference to David.

He wasn't angry at anything specific and wasn't looking for help. His life was out of control, and he felt it. He didn't care about God, friends, authority, or his own family. He was lashing out at the world and anyone or anything that tried to stop him. He didn't care about consequences. It was just selfish rage. It was obvious that this approach wasn't going to end well for him.

We got him off the church property that evening and took him home, but it was just another incident in a long chain of events. Over the next several years, we did the best we could with David, but it was nothing but an ongoing conflict. The kid had a police report as long as your arm.

One night, David was looking for some drugs and money to get high. This young man knew where his grandparents money and jewelry was hidden. He and a few of his friends, dressed in black and wearing ski masks, broke into his grandparent's trailer, beat them up, and stole what money they could find. With the ski masks on, his grandparents didn't recognize him. They pleaded for their assailants to take whatever they wanted and leave them alone, but David and his accomplices beat them anyway. They battered the elderly couple and stole whatever they could get their hands on. Yes, you read that right: he beat and robbed his own grandparents.

Just before they left the trailer that night, he made one mistake. Up to that point, he had remained silent behind the mask, but as he was leaving the trailer he said something to his grandparents, and they recognized his voice. When the police arrived, even though they had been beaten so severely they could barely move, they told the officers they knew who the robbers were. They turned in their own grandson.

A few months later, they testified at his trial. They described that night and how they recognized his voice. He was found guilty of breaking and entering with the intent to kill. This would be no juvenile lock up; the judge sentenced him to county prison.

The first night the guards took role call, they discovered this young man had ended up one cell down from the father he had never met.

And for the first time, David crossed paths with the man whose lifelong absence had driven him into a lifestyle of poor decisions. David had become just like the man he hated and resented.

I know that David's story is an extreme example. Not many kids are as wounded by the loss of their father or fall so far as he did. But the hurt is still there, and it is being multiplied millions of times over as fathers fail to be the godly parents their children need them to be.

Single moms, like David's, often do the best they can. Some are overwhelmed by the circumstances of life— perhaps working long hours, struggling to pay the bills, or caring for other children or elderly parents. Some have health problems of their own. Some have had limited educations or limited exposure to Christianity themselves. They drop their child off at a youth ministry, hoping that the leaders there can teach the kid right from wrong and help them turn out OK. David's mother was in desperate circumstances, raising a child alone while his father was in prison. She did the right thing by looking to the church to help her raise her son. But David needed a father. No matter how hard his mom tried, she couldn't fill that hole in his heart.

The youth pastor couldn't fill it either. No matter how much of a difference we can make as youth leaders, and I think it's a lot, we cannot become their parents. There are practical reasons, of course. We have a room full of kids. Every year some graduate, and there is a new bunch of incoming students to get to know. We only know a student for a few years, but family walks with them from birth to death. No matter how many overnights and trips we might take, we don't live with the child, waking and sleeping with them, sharing food, shelter, and clothing. Their father should be intertwined into the fabric of their daily life in ways we never can be. As much as the kid might respect and look up to us, they know that we are not a genuine authority figure in their life. We don't define who they are like their family does. A dad, a real dad, is there for them through all of life's ups and downs. We can never be.

And one more critical difference: everyone longs for approval from their father. What he thinks of us matters; it shapes the trajectory of our lives. As youth pastors, we can and often do affect the trajectories of the kids in our ministries. But we cannot replace the power of a dad to do great good or great harm in the life of a child.

And when the dad is absent and the mom is overwhelmed by the circumstances of life—including supporting a child as a single mom—she often looks to the church to make up the difference. But the family, not the youth ministry, is the primary influence in a child's life. While my heart breaks for broken families and while I wish that we could overcome that brokenness, the truth is that the youth leaders usually can't become replacement parents.

The children of America will never be healthy as long as the parents of America are as broken and divided as they are.

We can argue all day long about whose fault that is, but the bottom line is that we need intact marriages that model God's love and pass it on to their children.

In Deuteronomy 4:9, God told the parents of Israel to, "Watch yourselves closely so that you do not forget the things your eyes have seen or let them slip from your heart as long as you live. Teach them to your children and to their children after them." In Deuteronomy 11:18-19, He instructs parents to, "Fix these words of mine in your hearts and minds... Teach them to your children, talking about them when you sit at home and when you walk along the road, when you lie down and when you get up." God recognizes that the parent has primary responsibility for teaching their child right and wrong. We can support that with youth ministry, but we can't take its place. A child is shaped by their father and mother, and God knows that shaping can be positive or negative. In Ephesians 6:4, Paul writes that, "Fathers, do not exasperate your children; instead bring them up in the training and instruction of the Lord."

The book of Proverbs has a lot to say about parental discipline:

- "Whoever spares the rod hates their children,
  but the one who loves their children is careful to discipline them." (Proverbs 13:24).
- "Discipline your children, for in that there is hope;
  do not be a willing party to their death." (Proverbs 19:18).
- "Do not withhold discipline from a child;
  if you punish them with the rod, they will not die" (Proverbs 23:13).

- "Discipline your children, and they will give you peace; they will bring you the delights you desire" (Proverbs 29:17).

In the same vein, Hebrews 12:11 reminds us that, "No discipline seems pleasant at the time, but painful. Later on, however, it produces a harvest of righteousness and peace for those who have been trained by it." All of these verses suggest that parents who fail to discipline–for whatever reason–are doing harm to their children, leading them into the ways of sin and death. That comes off pretty harsh, but isn't that exactly what experience teaches us? A home without discipline, standards of moral behavior, or a compelling vision of what a good life looks like sets up a child to fail. Their failure is not inevitable, but with that sort of trajectory plotted for their life, the role of the youth pastor is to rescue the student, not raise them.

But what about parents who are beyond their capabilities because they were not raised well themselves? Do we ignore their plight? Of course not. We do everything that we can, within our sphere of influence, to set the student's life on the right course. The church as a whole might need to do more with the family to help the parent grow up and take leadership in the home.

But the point of this chapter is that one of the things that is limiting the effectiveness of youth ministry in America is that some parents, for whatever reason, expect youth pastors to do the job that only they can do. And while some of these parents are in desperate circumstances like David's mother was, others are just lazy. Raising a child is hard work; it takes enormous time and effort. For every David I've known in my ministry, I've encountered another student whose parents were just too self-absorbed to put in the effort. Or I've seen parents who wanted their child to be corrected, but weren't courageous enough to do it themselves. They wanted to play "good cop/bad cop," with me as the bad cop who told the kid what they couldn't do.

Youth ministry in America will remain limited in its effectiveness if a large number of parents abdicate their responsibility and expect the youth group to raise them. Somehow, some way, they need to solve their own problems and figure out how to raise children who know the love of a mother and a father. As youth pastors, we will do all we can to stand in the gap. But we can never really fill it.

Chapter 12

Undermining the Gospel at Home

Being a parent is the hardest job in America, especially today. Moms and dads have to provide for their children in a stressed economy. They must protect their kids from online influences and predators that they know nothing about and guard their hearts from a corrupting 24/7 media culture. They have to help with homework that they don't understand themselves, worry about health insurance, and pick up the pieces of their own broken families. They have to work more hours and still find time for parent-teacher conferences and their kids' sporting events. They are striving to be good examples and not hypocrites, often while trying to remedy their own hidden hurts. My heart breaks for parents that want to raise great kids but just feel overwhelmed and inadequate. The last thing I want to do is to make any parent feel even more burdened or inadequate.

But as much as Christian parents long for their children to become Christ-followers, they sometimes unintentionally undermine the progress of the Gospel in their own home. Some moms and dads are contradicting Jesus' message as they are taking their kids to church services, Sunday school programs, youth group nights, and Christian summer camps. I know parents who have undone the progress made in their son's or daughter's heart through a youth event during the car ride home. Kids learn very quickly that Jesus is what we talk about at church, not who we know and follow at home.

While we were serving one of our first churches in the late 1980s, Lori and I met some parents whose own emotional burnout was leaving a scar on their kids' souls. We inherited a ministry full of adolescents struggling with dysfunctional attitudes, rebellious spirits, and just plain nasty behaviors. Lori and I had no doubt about our responsibility and calling in that situation: to help those kids become like and follow Christ. We laid down loving but firm expectations for how they were to serve one another and respect the youth leaders. We practiced consistent discipleship and discipline. Our goal was to pour Jesus' love into the kids—even when it meant some moments of tough love—and to teach them to share that love with those around them. We thought the parents would be thrilled at the effort we put into their children's growth.

Unfortunately, the parents weren't thrilled. They were threatened and offended by the changes our ministry was making in their kids' behaviors. They began to push back and criticize our efforts, and Lori and I were hurt and confused. It felt like our new ministry was backfiring. Why were these moms and dads even bringing their kids to the youth ministry if they wanted them to remain spiritually immature? These parents interpreted the standards we were trying to set for their kids as a criticism of their own parenting methods. Even though the parents claimed to be Christians and were bringing their children to a Christian youth ministry, they didn't want us enforcing biblical standards for morality or speech in their kids' minds.

To give a simple example, we challenged the kids use of profanity. Not only did we not tolerate it at youth events, we explained why such speech was unworthy of Christ. Some kids seemed genuinely convicted and took what we said to heart. But there were some uncomfortable encounters when kids got picked up from youth group and their mom or dad started cussing like a sailor in the car on the way home. A few kids spoke up and shared what they had learned from Lori and I about unwholesome talk, and a few parents were embarrassed. But instead of being convicted in their own hearts and setting a better example for their kid, they resented the youth leaders for "interfering in their home."

These parents didn't understand what we were trying to do and interpreted our teaching as a lack of support for their parental authority. They would ask questions like, "Why are you trying to push Jesus on our kids?" or "Did we not do a good enough job raising them?" They criticized our teaching and even accused us of brainwashing their children.

We tried to assure them that we could not take their place and only wanted to walk with their teenagers, helping them grow into godly young men and women.

Lori and I were hurt by the criticism. We kept praying for wisdom so we could communicate with the home.

After all, Lori and I thought, isn't that our job? But some of these moms and dads began to speak up to the other adults at church, insisting that they knew exactly what they were doing as parents and the church had no business meddling in their family affairs.

While Lori and I were in the midst of the controversy, we had a hard time making sense of it. Our emotions were too raw. But over time, the Lord gave us a more spiritual perspective on what we—and so many others in ministry— went through. We remembered the parable Jesus told about a man sowing seeds (Matthew 13:1-23). In the story, some of the seeds fall on rocks, some fall on thorny soil, and some fall on good soil. The seeds represent God's word. Those that fall on rocky soil receive the word, but because there's no root, the seed fails to grow. The thorns represent worry and the deceitfulness of wealth, which choke out the life in the seed. A large part of youth ministry is helping clear the soil so that God can grow the fruits of the Spirit in teenagers. Youth leaders often have to do the hard work of clearing boulders and brambles or softening hard soil in a kid's heart so that the kid can even receive the Gospel. But sometimes, their family system is the obstacle to the seed taking root. It's hard for teenagers to believe in the love, joy, and peace that Jesus promised when many see fighting, distrust, anxiety, and sarcasm modeled at home. Youth pastors will preach a Gospel of freedom, but how can kids take it seriously when many see their parents enslaved to every kind of vice from workaholism to alcoholism?

Teenagers are not blind to hypocrisy. In fact, an age group searching for their identities is probably the one who can detect it the clearest. So when plank-eyed parents get upset at the specks they see in the eyes of their teenagers, the kids lose respect and trust for them and the Gospel they claim to follow. Jesus himself said, "A house divided against itself will fall" (Luke 11:17). Parents need to decide whether they will take a stand for the Gospel and uphold it by their actions or undermine every seed of the Gospel that the Church plants in their children by living a life contrary to the word. One of the bitterest truths any of us might need to swallow is that we are building a wall around our child's heart. And one of the most courageous and loving acts a parent can do is to admit that they need to become more spiritually mature so their child can see Jesus. It's also urgent because parents don't get that many years before their child is grown and living with the consequences of their example.

Lori and I were discouraged, but we refused to give up on our call to help these kids find and become more like Jesus. We endured the conflicts with as much grace as our young hearts had and tried to be as consistent with the adults as we were with their kids. We wanted them to see our hearts and that we weren't trying to undermine their parental rights. We wanted them to know that we honored the time they gave us with their kids by providing a biblically authentic youth ministry.

After about a year of trying to show the parents as much love as we showed the kids, God began to give us two wonderful types of fruit. First, some of the parents themselves came to Christ. God's Word came into their homes "out of the mouths of babes." Some were saved for the first time, and others were convicted by their own children's faith and rededicated their hearts to the Lord. Second, some of these same parents began to help us with the youth ministry.

I will never forget the parent open house we sponsored. Setting up a special night, we invited all the parents to come and see what the youth ministry was all about. Many came to the church frustrated, upset, and not knowing what was going to happen. As the night went on, we watched people engage in what we were teaching and how we supported the home and parents. When they left that night, they had a different opinion of us and how we ran things. It blew my mind. Some parents prayed with the youth leaders and found a personal relationship with Jesus Christ that very night. Young people were in awe of the power of God, and He used this to restore respect for our ministry. Everything had turned around–from comments like, "You're trying to brainwash our youth," to questions such as, "How can we serve this ministry?" There were parents who went on to volunteer in that youth ministry for ten years after that night, long after their own child had graduated. In the end, Lori and I were so thankful that God gave us the courage to stick with it and love parents despite their criticism.

Of course, not all parents are open to changing their ways and living out the Gospel in front of their kids. I remember a time at a church in Battle Creek, Michigan. We were hosting one of that summer's first youth events. We had food and fellowship, fun and games with more than 150 people and ended the night watching fireworks.

After the fireworks, we headed back to the church. A few kids were waiting for rides and were calling their parents to come and pick them up. One young lady was still waiting for a ride after everyone else had left. We called her mother and left a message. We waited, and the mom didn't show up or call back. We called over and over again but couldn't reach her. I was getting a little irritated and asked the young lady where she said her mother was going. Her response made me a little nervous. She said her mother was on a date with a guy she had just met a couple of weeks ago and would probably not be done with her date until well after midnight. The girl was only thirteen, and we couldn't drop her off at her house with no one home. So Lori and I did the best we could to entertain this young lady at the church while we waited for her mom.

Finally, well after 1 a.m., the mother showed up. Doing my best to show grace, I asked her why she had left her daughter (and us) sitting at the church for almost three hours. At this point, I was concerned for the well-being of this child, almost forgotten or abandoned by a mother whose own date with a new boyfriend was more important than her own daughter. As irritated as I was, I was also genuinely concerned for the mother. I asked the mom if she was OK, if she was hurt, or if something bad had happened that kept her from being back to pick up her daughter on time.

Her response was shockingly apathetic. She replied that she had been on a date with a new man and never expected to come back from a date before midnight. Frustrated by her attitude, I questioned why she had not even made the effort to let us know when to expect her. Then she got angry. She got in my face and began yelling, telling me that she didn't owe us anything, least of all any explanations for how she lived her life. She was distraught and defensive, insisting that we stay out of her business. She never thanked us for taking care of her daughter. That night, she cared for no one but herself.

From then on, the mother wanted nothing to do with the church. She pulled her daughter away from the youth ministry. We tried to follow up and build a relationship because we were concerned for both of them. The young girl badly wanted to come back to the youth group, but the mother wouldn't allow her to return to the church. The girl's friends often asked why she couldn't come back, and her response was that her mother didn't care for the church and the way that we handled the situation that night. In the mother's mind, we had driven her and her daughter away from the church.

About five years later, we saw this young girl at a mall. Lori and I didn't recognize her at first, but when we did, we were eager to hear how her life had been going. She told us that her mother had gotten pregnant by the man she dated that night and that he left her a year later. She talked about how she begged her mother to come back to the church but was never able to change her mother's mind.

Then the girl, following her mother's example, got pregnant herself when she was fifteen, just over a year after leaving the church. As we sat in the mall, she told us in tears how her friends were unable to reach her because of her bitterness. She talked about how much her life changed over those next few years and how she wished she would've just had one more opportunity to come back to church and be a part of what God had for her life. She loved her friends at the church, but she couldn't understand why her mother continued to keep her away. About a year later, her mother got married again. The next year she got a divorce. This was the mother's third marriage. Some things never change. Sin runs deep. Generational sin runs deeper. It didn't change the fact that her daughter will have scars and pain from never coming back to the very thing she loved. Now this young lady, at the age of eighteen, is raising a child by herself, and her mother will not allow her to live at the house. She currently stays with another family. I truly believe that one decision by her mother to not pick her daughter up on time led to a cascade of events that changed her life.

Throughout my career in youth ministry, I have seen parents over and over again undermine the work of the Gospel in their children's lives. Some parents might bring their kids to a youth group, but their own hearts are ignorant, arrogant, and thoughtless of the effect they are having on their kids.

God entrusts parents with a huge responsibility, and parenting can be a beautiful, fulfilling thing.

It's up to Christian parents to put their kids in places, like youth group, where they can hear the Gospel message. But perhaps what's even more important is for these parents to live out the Gospel of love in their day to day lives so that their children can truly understand it.

Chapter 13

Jesus Freaks

Some parents want their kid to go to youth group to learn good values, respect for authority, and decent behavior. They just don't want their kids going off the deep end and turning into Jesus freaks.

In one of our first youth ministries, we inherited two young people from a very dysfunctional home. The parents did not go to church nor did they want their two adolescents going to church. Our congregation ran an outreach ministry campaign in a very distressed area of downtown Battle Creek, Michigan. This neighborhood had a reputation as one of the poorest and roughest communities in the city. After a few days of outreach meetings, we had seen many teens come to Jesus.

Now that these kids had accepted Christ, we wanted to get them involved in various ministries for discipleship, fellowship, education, service, etc. But these kids didn't have transportation to our church campus in another part of Battle Creek. I wasn't going to let this be an obstacle, so we arranged rides for the kids back and forth to our campus for various ministries throughout the week.

As we began to drive youth back and forth from church, after a few months, it became clear that these young people's lives had been radically changed by their new walk with Christ. They discovered that Jesus loved them for who they were, and it didn't matter where they lived. They were enjoying a new sense of spiritual freedom, moral responsibility, and the joy of serving others. Those of us who worked with them were thrilled by what God was doing in their lives. They wanted to matter for him.

So the youth ministry staff was totally unprepared for the backlash we encountered and where it came from. I had seen and heard of plenty of examples where kids that came from rough backgrounds were unwelcome in the church, but I'd never met parents that were opposed to their own children loving God too much. The resistance we met was from the parents of these inner city teens, who were upset that these young people were spending so much time with us at church. At first, I thought it was because of a cultural gap or because they distrusted us. But over time, I realized that these parents were upset that their kids were becoming too Christian. Their kids were turning away from their parents' and communities' values, and they choose to align themselves with God's Kingdom. Their parents felt that as rejection, and they were hurt that their kids were slipping away from their influence.

I can understand how they must have felt. Our intent was never to drive a wedge between these kids and their folks. But turning to Christ often does mean beginning a process of turning away from the world that raised you. It can also introduce conflict in relationships that straddle the divide.

Jesus had a lot to say about this. Over and over in the gospels, he talks about the cost of following him and how it will often divide families:

> "Do not suppose that I have come to bring peace to the earth. I did not come to bring peace, but a sword. For I have come to turn
> 'a man against his father,
> a daughter against her mother,
> a daughter-in-law against her mother-in-law—
> a man's enemies will be the members of his own household.'

"Anyone who loves their father or mother more than me is not worthy of me; anyone who loves their son or daughter more than me is not worthy of me. Whoever does not take up their cross and follow me is not worthy of me." (Matthew 10:34-38)

Large crowds were traveling with Jesus, and turning to them He said: "If anyone comes to me and does not hate father and mother, wife and children, brothers and sisters—yes, even their own life—such a person cannot be my disciple. And whoever does not carry their cross and follow me cannot be my disciple." (Luke 14:25-27)

"Truly I tell you," Jesus replied, "no one who has left home or brothers or sisters or mother or father or children or fields for me and the gospel will fail to receive a hundred times as much in this present age: homes, brothers, sisters, mothers, children and fields—along with persecutions—and in the age to come eternal life." (Mark 10:29-30)

Many parents are afraid of the possible side effects of youth discipleship. Yes, they want their kids to develop discipline and moral behavior, but they don't want passion for Christ. They get really uncomfortable when their kids pray out loud in restaurants before meals or want to go preach the Gospel in sketchy downtown neighborhoods. They would much rather have quiet, moralistic adolescents who submit to their every demand without question.

While the Gospel will certainly produce morals and obedience in the youth, love is its ultimate goal. And Jesus won't settle for a passionless love.

Let's look at some of His words:

"Love the Lord your God with all your heart and with all your soul and with all your mind and with all your strength." (Mark 12:30)

Then he said to them all: "Whoever wants to be my disciple must deny themselves and take up their cross daily and follow me." (Luke 9:23)

And John's words from the book of Revelation:

I know your deeds, that you are neither cold nor hot. I wish you were either one or the other! So, because you are lukewarm—neither hot nor cold— I am about to spit you out of my mouth.
(Revelation 3:15-16)

Yes, it's scary to let kids go minister to homeless drug addicts and gang members. But what happens when they start to produce supernatural love and joy in their lives from living out the Gospel? Is it right to stamp those seeds out in order to secure their safety? Is it even possible to contain the love of God when it comes bursting out of the seams of one's life?

Like skydiving, living out the Gospel is not something you can do halfway. Either you take the leap of faith or stay onboard contemplating the pros and cons until the plane lands and you've missed the opportunity.

One day, when we were doing another project in that same Battle Creek location, we went to the homes of some of these newly born-in-Christ young people. We offered to help their parents by doing some repairs and light construction work in their homes. They were blown away that we would even take time to come and help them fix walls and broken windows that needed repair. We started supplying lunches and dinner for the families.

As we spent a few days in this home, the parents came to realize we cared and they were moved by our love. In those few months of connecting with their teens and now serving their families, they had no problem allowing their youth to be a part of our ministry. They saw past the narrow vision of what they thought the church was and began to experience what the church was really all about: Christ's hand extended.

After years of relationship building and working in that area, we won many youth to the Lord and connected with many families in that community. We developed a Christ-like relationship with the entire block of families. They began to send all their young people to church, and then the parents started coming. It was a great win for both the Church and Battle Creek. "One young person at a time" became our new philosophy for what God had called us to do. In a few short years, our outreach to the community was more than just "look what the church can do;" it became "look at what Christ can do."

Yet none of this would have happened had we not taken the time to invest. If we had ignored this call and let the love of Christ in us grow stagnant, the area would not have experienced him in the way they did. We cannot stop the youth from carrying out Christ's mission for this world just because we are uncomfortable with it. We need to get onboard with Jesus' plan to revive this earth. Because the ultimate vision for youth ministry is not to have a bunch of kids sitting around a church building eating pizza and half-listening to a sermon.

It's doing what Jesus did: training young people in the ways of love and then sending them out into the world to establish His kingdom.

That kind of discipleship will always cause division. It will divide communities and families. When someone is born again in Christ, they are a new creation and are set onto a new path. But there is a difference between division as a result of following Christ and the ministry being divisive. We are not calling youth to leave their families to join a cult. We are helping Christ bring life and hope through them to their families, homes, and schools. Sometimes that will result in resistance, but it need not always be. If we train young people to be followers of Christ, to exhibit his character, they won't be "Jesus Freaks." They will be authentic Christians, released into this world to represent the Father's love and extend the Kingdom of God. Isn't that the whole point of youth ministry?

Chapter 14

Why it's Worth It

Youth ministry is exhausting.

That's not exactly what they put on the front of the Bible college brochure trying to convince someone to get a degree in youth ministry. It's not a winning sales pitch when you recruit volunteer youth workers. It won't be the title of the most popular workshop session at a youth ministry conference. But it's honest. I've been doing this for twenty-seven years. I've never considered doing anything else for a living, and I've never aspired to being a senior pastor. I know what my calling is and what career I am cut out for. So take it from me because I have been around the block more times than I can count. Youth ministry will make you tired, bone tired, sometimes.

Why? Because it requires irregular hours and a never-ending schedule of rallies, retreats, car washes, late night phone calls, breakfast meetings, Saturday night emergencies, teenage crises, loud music, and games with kids who have more energy than you can ever remember having.

Aside from trying to keep up with the kids, youth pastors carry the stress of managing a budget, building strong parental relationships, providing for their own families on a youth pastor's salary, and trying to understand teens' constantly changing world. Some days it leaves you so worn out you don't think you can go on.

Ultimately, every youth pastor has to ask him or herself two simple questions: *Why do I do this?* and, *Is this worth it?* Personally, I could be doing a lot of things—landscaping, coaching, carpentering, teaching. Yet here I am.

Why? It's worth it because of who Christ is. There is nothing more satisfying to me than taking a kid who society or culture or family says is a piece of junk and showing him or her life abundant in Christ and how beautiful he or she is in God's sight. This happens over and over again, and every time, the words of Isaiah 61 resonate through me, strong and true:

> *The Spirit of the Sovereign LORD is on me,*
> *because the LORD has anointed me*
> *to proclaim good news to the poor.*

He has sent me to bind up the brokenhearted,
to proclaim freedom for the captives
and release from darkness for the prisoners,
to proclaim the year of the LORD's favor
and the day of vengeance of our God,
to comfort all who mourn,
and provide for those who grieve in Zion—
to bestow on them a crown of beauty
instead of ashes,
the oil of joy
instead of mourning,
and a garment of praise
instead of a spirit of despair.
They will be called oaks of righteousness,
a planting of the LORD
for the display of his splendor.
(Isaiah 61:1-3)

Youth ministry is worth it to me because I want to leave a lasting impact for Christ on these kids. I want to be like Peter in Acts, who walked so fully in the truth of the Lord that his mere shadow would heal people. I want to walk in faith like Paul, who ran down three flights of stairs to bring a kid back to life.

It's worth it to me when I get to see the greatest miracle of all: God's transformation in an individual's life and heart. It's worth it when I reflect on the story of a young man in Battle Creek, Michigan who had no connection with his biological father. This kid was very distant from his stepfather, floundering in his relationship with Christ, and had no purpose or plan when he came into my ministry. I had the privilege and joy of telling him how God wanted to use him in huge ways. This kid became the worship leader for the youth group and its choir director. He graduated and went on to Bible college. Afterwards, I officiated at his wedding to a young lady from the youth group. This young man became like spiritual son to me. He went on to to start a youth ministry in Cleveland. Today, he is the youth pastor at the church where he started in Battle Creek. God brought him full circle.

It's worth it when you go to the hospital and get to nurture and guide a young lady horrified over the death of a family member. Seeing her become better and not bitter and watching her perspective change to believing that God has a purpose and plan for all things shows me that I am doing something worthwhile.

It's worth it when you have a niece who—when told she has cancer in the ninth grade and that it would require her leg to be amputated—tells herß family, "This does not define me. I will persevere, and I will rise up because of God." Today, she's in her final year of college, studying to be a nurse.

It's worth it to see young people's lives transformed by the power of God.

It's worth it to make beauty out of the ashes when a young lady walks up to you and says she's adopted and making really poor choices. It's worth it when I get to tell her the truth: that God is her father, and He loved her so much that He gave her two sets of parents and grandparents. It's worth it to see her disposition change when I say, "You are extra blessed." I love speaking life, taking tragedy and turning it into triumph, garbage into grace.

The apostle Paul got tired, sometimes. He worked hard and suffered much. He did it for Christ, he did it for the Gospel, and he did it because he loved the people he ministered to. He considered his life nothing if he could not spread the grace of God in the lives of those broken by sin. Earlier in this chapter, I listed some of the demands put upon youth pastors: late hours, loud music, etc. But consider what Paul endured for the love of his ministry:

> Are they servants of Christ? (I am out of my mind to talk like this.) I am more. I have worked much harder, been in prison more frequently, been flogged more severely, and been exposed to death again and again. Five times I received from the Jews the forty lashes minus one. Three times I was beaten with rods, once I was pelted with stones, three times I was shipwrecked, I spent a night and a day in the open sea, I have been constantly on the move. I have been in danger from rivers, in danger from bandits, in danger from my fellow Jews, in danger from Gentiles; in danger in the city, in danger in the country, in danger at sea; and in danger from false believers. I have labored and toiled and have often gone

*without sleep; I have known hunger and thirst
and have often gone without food; I have been
cold and naked. Besides everything else, I face
daily the pressure of my concern for all the
churches. Who is weak, and I do not feel weak?
Who is led into sin, and I do not inwardly burn?
(2 Corinthians 11:23-29)*

I'm glad that you're reading this book. I hope that it
inspires and helps you and that you tell your friends about
it so that they buy one too. I wouldn't be honest if I didn't
say that I'd like to sell a lot of copies. But the success of my
ministry won't be measured by how few or how many I
sell. It's not about books and conferences and recognition,
and it certainly isn't about making money (especially in
youth ministry).

It is about making it matter. It is about being relevant
to the Kingdom, even if that means being irrelevant to the
world and its culture. It is not about seeing crowds of
students wearing T-shirts with your name on them but
about seeing students as individual young men and
women with God-given worth and potential. It's about
giving them hope and a future in Christ. It is about being
an instrument in God's hands to place His mark on their

lives. And the only way to do that is to care enough to engage with them. To get close enough to them to make a difference, we have to be at those events where the music seems too loud, the kids too energetic, and the teenage angst too dramatic. We have to go on another weekend retreat or meet a kid in crisis at one in the morning. We have to attend their school events and sports, and occasionally meet them at the police station when they get into trouble. Yes, youth ministry is tiring, but exhaustion is a price I will pay to help kids become the people God calls them to be.

How did Paul measure success? Was it in degrees or awards or in the books he wrote? Did he consider his ministry validated because he got to speak at conferences or was recognized by denominational officials? No, Paul said that the only endorsements or recommendations that he needed were written on the hearts of the people he ministered to:

> *Are we beginning to commend ourselves again? Or do we need, like some people, letters of recommendation to you or from you? You yourselves are our letter, written on our hearts, known and read by everyone. You show that you*

are a letter from Christ, the result of our ministry, written not with ink but with the Spirit of the living God, not on tablets of stone but on tablets of human hearts. (2 Corinthians 3:1-3)

I know a pastor who has preached the Gospel to students for twenty-five years, on several continents. He wasn't raised a Christian. When he was a teenager, he was aimless and rebellious. He went to a few youth ministry concerts and rallies, but he always sat in the back row, just a part of the crowd. It wasn't until a few years later, as he was nearing the end of his college years, that someone got close enough to him to reach him for Christ, and it changed the course of his life. But when I think of him as a sixteen or seventeen year-old young man, blending into the crowd at a Jesus concert, I become even more determined to get to know the kids on the edges of the events.

How many of them have gifts and callings, just waiting to be discovered?

Anybody can complain about anything at any time (especially youth ministry), but it takes genuine character to rise above frustration and exhaustion and discouragement. It's worth it. I have chosen to devote my career to youth ministry, no matter how tiring it can be sometimes. God didn't let me go down the same road as my earthly father. He gave me a different path. Though it is narrow, it has been more than worth it to follow him as he leads me down righteous paths and beside quiet waters.

Chapter 15

Is There Hope for Youth Ministry in America?

With all of the challenges we face in reaching the next generation, along with all the changes and challenges we face in our churches, can we reasonably hope that youth ministries will remain a potent force in American culture ten or twenty years from now?

Let me start my answer by sharing the last thing Jesus said to his disciples, the fledgling Church, right before he ascended to heaven, a few weeks before Pentecost:

> *Then Jesus came to them and said, "All authority in heaven and on earth has been given to me. Therefore go and make disciples of all nations, baptizing them in the name of the Father and of the Son and of the Holy Spirit, and teaching them to obey everything I have commanded you. And*

surely I am with you always, to the very end of the age." (Matthew 28:18-20)

Read the above paragraph again, and notice what Jesus says:

"All authority on heaven and earth has been given to me." That means no matter how big the problems are that we face, Jesus is bigger.

No matter how much cultural change and spiritual warfare impact the next generation and our ministries, Jesus is powerful enough to overcome them.

We have nothing to be afraid of. We are to be like David, who wasn't afraid when he stood looking up at the giant Goliath because he saw a bigger God looking down on the Philistine. Yes, we have our work cut out for us in youth ministry today. But we have all the help we need, if we will rely on the King.

"Therefore go and make disciples of all nations, baptizing them in the name of the Father and of the Son and of the Holy Spirit, and teaching them to obey everything I have commanded you." Our task in youth ministry is the same as the task for the Church in general: find the lost, lead them to Christ, and help them grow to become faithful followers of Jesus. We aren't here to win the approval of people or of teens. We are here to win the approval of God by doing His work. Our youth ministries should operate on the Great Commission: make more and better followers of Christ.

"And surely I am with you always, to the very end of the age." Is there hope for youth ministry? To even ask the question is to doubt Jesus' promise in this passage. Two thousand years ago and half a planet away, He sent us into the world. He has never abandoned His Church, and He never will. Yes, there have been challenging times, even periods of suffering and persecution. But He never abandoned His people during those times, and He never abandons His Church as it faithfully carries out its mission. So yes, there is hope for youth ministry in

America as long as we rely on the presence and promise of Jesus.

But here's what cannot happen with our youth ministries: we cannot continue to make the mistakes of the Laodiceans. Laodicea was a city in Asia Minor during the days of the New Testament Church. It was a center of Christianity in that region. In Revelation 3, Jesus has John write a letter to this church, sharing what Christ thought of their ministry. Here's what he had to say to the Laodicean christians:

"To the angel of the church in Laodicea write:

These are the words of the Amen, the faithful and true witness, the ruler of God's creation. I know your deeds, that you are neither cold nor hot. I wish you were either one or the other! So, because you are lukewarm—neither hot nor cold—I am about to spit you out of my mouth. You say, 'I am rich; I have acquired wealth and do not need a thing.' But you do not realize that you are wretched, pitiful, poor, blind and naked. I counsel you to buy from me gold refined in the fire, so you can become rich; and white clothes to wear, so you can cover your shameful nakedness; and salve to put on your eyes, so you can see.

Those whom I love I rebuke and discipline. So be earnest and repent. Here I am! I stand at the door and knock. If anyone hears my voice and opens the door, I will come in and eat with that person, and they with me.

To the one who is victorious, I will give the right to sit with me on my throne, just as I was victorious and sat down with my Father on His throne. Whoever has ears, let them hear what the Spirit says to the churches." (Revelation 3:14-22)

They were a wealthy church with all that money could buy. And yet, Christ was disappointed with them because their hearts and ministries were neither hot nor cold. They had no passion for the Gospel. They went through the motions, and they felt pretty good about themselves. But in reality, they were spiritually bankrupt.

Are our youth ministries like the Laodiceans? Are we not wealthy with church buildings, programs, buses, staff, and a thousand technological toys? But do we go through the motions of youth ministry without genuine passion for the Gospel? If youth ministry in America is in trouble, it's not because the youth are lukewarm; it's because we are. We need to stop blaming the kids and start saving them.

Here's what I believe: Jesus is saving the best for last.

That's what he did at the wedding at Cana. Remember how they had run out of wine? Jesus' mother Mary asked him if he could do something about the problem, as it was an embarrassment to the host and a frustration for the guests:

> Nearby stood six stone water jars, the kind used by the Jews for ceremonial washing, each holding from twenty to thirty gallons.
> Jesus said to the servants, "Fill the jars with water," so they filled them to the brim.
> Then he told them, "Now draw some out and take it to the master of the banquet."

They did so, and the master of the banquet tasted the water that had been turned into wine. He did not realize where it had come from, although the servants who had drawn the water knew. Then he called the bridegroom aside and said, "Everyone brings out the choice wine first and then the cheaper wine after the guests have had too much to drink; but you have saved the best till now." (John 2:6-10)

There is a pattern in the Christian life: when our resources and hope is depleted, when we believe that we can't succeed or survive, God often chooses to act. When things look darkest, He dawns. He brings beauty from ashes. This is the heart of His messianic ministry, a ministry of redemption to a dying world. As He prophesies in Isaiah 61:

The Spirit of the Sovereign LORD is on me,
because the LORD has anointed me
to proclaim good news to the poor.
He has sent me to bind up the brokenhearted,
to proclaim freedom for the captives
and release from darkness for the prisoners,

to proclaim the year of the LORD's favor
and the day of vengeance of our God,
to comfort all who mourn,
and provide for those who grieve in Zion—
to bestow on them a crown of beauty
instead of ashes,
the oil of joy
instead of mourning,
and a garment of praise
instead of a spirit of despair.
They will be called oaks of righteousness,
a planting of the LORD
for the display of His splendor.
(Isaiah 61:1-3)

Those verses were written about Jesus, but they apply to those of us who follow Him and do his work in youth ministry. Are you discouraged? I know I've written these words here before, but I know the word of God can be an encouragement. Then really listen to what He says. The spirit of the sovereign Lord is upon your youth ministry because He has anointed you to proclaim good news to the poor—the poor teenagers who are children of divorce, the poor kids who were raised on meaningless video games, the poor kids who were raised in poverty, the poor kids that have fallen into drugs, sex, gangs, and violence because those were a part of the culture they grew up in, and they knew nothing else. He has sent your youth ministry to bind up this brokenhearted generation, to proclaim their freedom from all the evil and empty things that have held them captive, and to release them from the darkness of lives leading them to Hell.

He has sent your youth ministry to proclaim that this season in history is the year of the Lord's favor in which God can and will do great things. He wants your youth ministry to teach them that the Lord will take vengeance on evil and comfort all those who have been victimized by it.

He has sent your youth ministry to provide for those who grieve in our churches over their children who have left our congregations and seem to be wandering without Christ in their lives. He has sent your youth ministry to reach out to kids that the world thinks are useless and place on them a crown of beauty as you anoint them with the grace and salvation of Christ. He has sent your youth ministry to turn this generation's despair to praise.

And when—not if, but when—your youth ministry really makes it matter by refusing to be relevant to a dying culture and instead raise these kids up to be relevant to God's Kingdom, then those lost boys and girls will grow into oaks of righteousness, leaders of the next generation Church in America. They will be a planting of the Lord, for his glory and splendor.

Do I believe there is hope for youth ministry in America? If youth pastors will heed God's call to fulfill the Great Commission upon the mission field of teenage America, there is more than hope ahead. There is glory.

Conclusion: It's Time to be [ir]Relevant

What do today's teens need? Maybe that's too big of a question. Let me be more specific: what do they need from us? OK, the answer to that problem is probably a pretty long list. Let me be even more specific. Who do these teens need us to be?

Well, let's start by considering that the 2010 United States Census found that 27% of American kids are growing up in single parent homes. In urban areas, it's over 50%. Let's also consider that most of those single parents are moms, and that even in homes with two parents, fathers are not the strong influences that they used to be in earlier generations. In general, fathers are not a strong influence in our culture. On television and in the movies, they are normally portrayed as either abusive or clueless or as buffoons. Generation Y—the Millennials— has been shaped by all sorts of influences. We usually point to how much technology they grew up with, but I think that we ought to reflect on how few positive male role models they've had in their lives.

So when you ask me who they need us to be, I'd say that they don't need us to be their big brothers, their cool uncles, or their older buddies. What they need are fathers. We can't be their dads, but we can represent the Father to them, and point them to Him. They need His love and His strength because too many of them have never experienced the compassion, courage, and justice of a godly man.

Do they need us to be relevant to their pop culture? They get that every day, all day. Better that we offer them what the world doesn't and never will, because it can't.

I know all the reasons why youth ministry ought to be "relevant." I can make those arguments—in fact, at times in my career I have. For example, I would have argued that Paul himself made his ministry relevant to whatever group or culture he was reaching out to. In 1 Corinthians 9:19-22, he says:

> ...I have made myself a slave to everyone, to win as many as possible. To the Jews I became like a Jew, to win the Jews. To those under the law I

became like one under the law (though I myself am not under the law), so as to win those under the law. To those not having the law I became like one not having the law...so as to win those not having the law. To the weak I became weak, to win the weak. I have become all things to all people so that by all possible means I might save some. (1 Corinthians 9:19-22)

I also would have said that Paul was imitating Jesus, whose ministry was "incarnational:" he went where the lost were, lived among them, and spoke their language. I would have pointed out how many great missionaries brought the faith to distant corners of the world by imitating Christ's incarnational ministry. Shouldn't we at least do the same with our own teens? Why wouldn't we want to incarnate Christ in their subculture?

A youth pastor friend of mine named Steve told me about an incident, which made him think about what cultural relevance meant. Here's how he explained it:

"Back a few years ago, Rock Band and Guitar Hero were the rage and everyone was playing. Like many youth ministries, we had a small video game area, so I figured I'd set up Rock Band for our students to play. It took all of two weeks for my phone to start ringing. Apparently, one of the leaders in our church came to drop off his kids and instead of hearing the sounds of praise and worship, he was blasted with "Free Bird" or some other Lynyrd Skynyrd guitar solo. Filled with the images of a misspent youth, this leader took his kids and left. His calls, and my lead pastor's calls, soon followed.

"These are the seemingly insignificant moments that I'm talking about. They aren't broadcast for everyone to hear. But make no mistake: these type of things don't stay quiet. I had a decision to make. Would I allow my pride to puff me up? Would I stick to my guns and defend my position of youth relevance and evangelistic ambiance? Would I draw my sword to fight or fall? Or would I listen to the still small voice of the Holy Spirit and put people above pride?

"I look back on that night of phone calls, and thank God I chose the latter. Make no mistake, the choice wasn't between having a video game or not. It was about my ability to pastor a family and his boys. I told my pastor that night, "I'm not going to fall on my sword for Rock Band," and I meant that and more. That statement has rung true multiple times in my ministry. In ministry there are only a few things for which it is worth "falling on your sword:" the un-compromised Gospel, the call of Christ to reach our world, and the privilege to lead your flock in their pursuit of Christ. Guard those things at all cost. Draw your sword to fight or fall when necessary and pray God would give you wisdom to discern the rest."

On my career journey through youth ministry, I have come to believe that whenever we have to choose, we should choose to be relevant to God's Kingdom rather than contemporary culture.

Yes, we want to be incarnational, but we also want to be prophetic, to call kids to Christ by offering them something their culture can't.

The message is the medium. If we have to "sell" Christ by reducing him to a pop culture afterthought or icon, we have communicated what matters most to us. Christ matters most to me, and He should matter most to the kids. We need to make it matter.

Besides, if pop-culturally relevant youth ministry works, why are there fewer and fewer kids coming to Christ and joining the Church through it? We have spent the last twenty to thirty years trying to be as cool as we can to draw a crowd. How has that worked out? Read the statistics in the introduction of this book.

Yes, teens today need to know that Jesus cares about them and their problems. And so we present a savior who appears to have nothing better to do than hang out with teens, immersed in their world. But they also need to know that Jesus has the power to do something about those problems. To do that, we need them to hear His call to leave behind the aspects of their culture that are unworthy and join His Kingdom. Our ministries need to be irrelevant to the culture of a world that is perishing but relevant to the things that endure.

Rather than instructing us to distort the Gospel to relate to the world, Peter calls us to become gloriously and prophetically irrelevant. "Dear friends, I urge you, as foreigners and exiles, to abstain from sinful desires, which wage war against your soul. Live such good lives among the pagans that, though they accuse you of doing wrong, they may see your good deeds and glorify God on the day he visits us" (1 Peter 2:11-12). Nor does Paul tell us to relate our thinking and ministries to the pattern of the world. He opposes pop culture, saying, "Do not conform to the pattern of this world, but be transformed by the renewing of your mind. Then you will be able to test and approve what God's will is—His good, pleasing and perfect will" (Romans 12:2).

When I was the Youth Alive Director for the state of Michigan from 1999-2001, I traveled to secular high school campuses all across the state to plant prayer clubs. I was especially proud of the plants we made in the Detroit area. We helped establish a Youth Alive club at almost half of the schools we visited. At one of them, Crestwood High School, 67% of the students were Muslim. It wasn't the kind of school that normally supports a flourishing Christian youth ministry. But I knew two things: Crestwood needed Christ, and it would take a very special person to lead a group there.

The leader we placed at Crestwood was a young lady who I was certain would continually challenge the students to see Jesus Christ for who he really was. She wasn't the kind of person who would try to "sell" Christ by watering down His identity and message to make it "relevant" to either the secular or Muslim cultures. I also knew she wouldn't reduce the ministry to a militant bickering match with the Muslim majority. I felt confident in her character because of how she ended up at Crestwood in the first place. This was her first year there. She had grown up in Christian schools. But the previous summer, I had spoken at a youth camp. That evening, I had challenged the students to reach their campuses for Christ. She came up to me afterword with a determined look in her eyes. She said that she had accepted my challenge, but since she was attending a Christian high school, she felt that her opportunity for ministry was more limited (of course, not all students at a Christian school are Christians, but she wanted a bigger mission field). She told me that she was determined to transfer to a secular school where the need was greatest. The next day, she asked her parents if she could go to Crestwood. They were skeptical at first. But they had raised her to love God and obey his leadings. They said that if she was sure that the Lord was calling her to Crestwood, they wouldn't hold her back.

That fall she started the prayer club at Crestwood. I continued my traveling, and didn't see her for the rest of the fall. But in January, I came back through and visited the area again. We held a big after-school party in the gym, and hundreds of students came. After a while, I got up and gave a short message, and I used it to share God's word with them, challenging them to follow Christ. At the end of the event, I asked the club leader to stand up and be introduced to lots of teens whom she didn't know. I shared how faithful she had been, speaking every week into the lives of the students at Crestwood. As she stood there, over sixty students thanked God and her for her leadership. One by one, they got up and shared how this young lady had lead them into a personal relationship with Jesus Christ.

This was the first Christian club to even get a toehold at Crestwood. But she had done more than that, she had succeeded. She had begun with prayer, and in just a few months, she built a dynamic ministry that was changing eternal destinies. She was expanding the Kingdom on a campus where two-thirds of the students were Muslim. Before she had graduated, she had led hundreds of Crestwood students to Christ, including some Muslims.

Before she left Crestwood, I asked her what she wanted to do with the rest of her life. Her answer? "I want your job. Someday, I want to plant prayer clubs on campuses all across America."

I want her to. We need her to. Because this young woman gets it. She understands that the high school campuses of America don't need more relevance to pop culture. The students don't need to be condescended and pandered to. They don't need more culturally sensitive outreach that apologizes or minimizes the distinctive message of the Gospel. They need a Savior who is gloriously, wondrously irRevelevant to a culture of moral decay and spiritual despair. They need a Father that loves them and would give his first born son for them. They need Jesus.

After twenty-seven years in youth ministry, I can tell you that it is worth it.

Every youth pastor has moments that remind him that this is important work, worth dedicating a life to do. Here is one of those people. This is from an email that a teenage girl in New Jersey wrote me after I spoke at a retreat there:

"I was at the retreat you preached at on the 5th, 6th, and 7th. I just wanted to let you know that at that retreat,

God really broke me down. I had a lot of hate, anger, and depression built up in my heart. So much that there was no room for God. [So] I had no idea what love really was. I was searching to find it in all the wrong places. Through alcohol, popping pills, and relationships. I was hurt and confused for eight years of my life.

"This retreat was my breakthrough. I was sitting at the altar on Saturday night crying, tired of being an alcoholic and a pill popper at fifteen years old. I was thinking about where the source of all of these things came from, [and it] stirred up the anger and the hatred again. All of a sudden, I felt this warm presence all over my body; my mind was cleared from all of the hurt. I had no idea what was happening to me. I asked God what was going on, and I could hear him say, "Love."

"That night I gave my heart to God completely. I laid everything down at the altar and surrendered myself to God. I finally knew what Love was, and through Love comes forgiveness. It was hard to do, but God showed me how to forgive my brother and to show Love to him. Now I am a changed, re-arranged, strong woman of God. I know not to turn back to my old ways of looking for love, because the only place I'll find it is when I'm seeking and following God."

Randy DonGiovanni

—Kate, South New Jersey

After reading this book, I hope and pray that you will do three things. First, commit yourself to making it matter, to doing ministry that relates to God's Kingdom more than the world. Second, care about youth ministry for its own sake, not just as a rung that you need to climb on your career ladder so you can get to more prestigious roles within the Church. Finally, rejoice because Jesus loves you and has called you to love kids in his name. Could there be a better job?

About the Author

Randy DonGiovanni: Randy is a graduate of Valley Forge Christian College in Phoenixville, PA. He also attended West Chester University in West Chester, PA.

Randy and Lori have worked with youth and young adults for over twenty-seven years. In addition, Randy was the former Speed-the-Light and Youth Alive Director in the state of Michigan.

He has experience in speaking to students at rallies, retreats, camps, high school, and college campuses all over the nation.

Randy has a sincere desire and vision is to be used by the Lord in seeing lives radically changed for the kingdom of God. Through practical application of scripture, humor, and story-telling, Randy motivates and encourages young people to live a committed and Spirit-filled life.

For more information about RandyDon Ministries, please visit Randy's website at randydon.org.

Made in the USA
Monee, IL
19 April 2021

65173037R00121